PRENTICE HALL

·MAGRUDER'S·
AMERICAN
GOVERNMENT

Test Prep
Workbook for
American Government

PEARSON
Prentice
Hall

Needham, Massachusetts
Upper Saddle River, New Jersey

ISBN 0-13-128397-9

3 4 5 6 7 8 9 10   08 07 06 05

CONTENTS

PART I

Part I consists of multiple-choice tests arranged unit by unit.

PART II

Part II consists of three separate exams: one that covers a typical first semester, one that covers a typical second semester, and one that covers a whole course.

PART III

Part III consists of study sheets arranged unit by unit.

Taking Tests

Do you panic at the thought of taking a standardized test? Here are some tips that most test developers recommend to help you achieve good scores.

MULTIPLE-CHOICE QUESTIONS

Read each part of a multiple-choice question to make sure you understand what is being asked.

Many tests are made up of multiple-choice questions. Some multiple-choice items are **direct questions.** They are complete sentences followed by possible answers, called distractors.

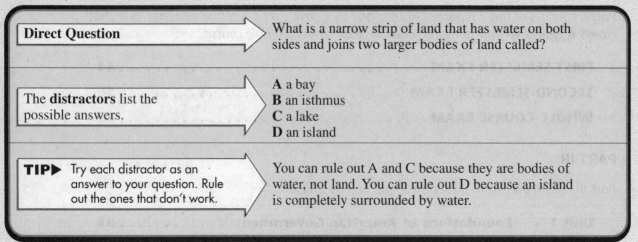

Direct Question → What is a narrow strip of land that has water on both sides and joins two larger bodies of land called?

The **distractors** list the possible answers. →
A a bay
B an isthmus
C a lake
D an island

TIP▶ Try each distractor as an answer to your question. Rule out the ones that don't work. → You can rule out A and C because they are bodies of water, not land. You can rule out D because an island is completely surrounded by water.

Other multiple-choice questions are **incomplete sentences** that you are to finish. They are followed by possible answers.

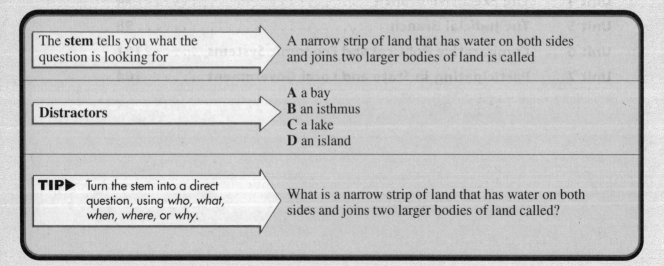

The **stem** tells you what the question is looking for → A narrow strip of land that has water on both sides and joins two larger bodies of land is called

Distractors →
A a bay
B an isthmus
C a lake
D an island

TIP▶ Turn the stem into a direct question, using *who, what, when, where,* or *why.* → What is a narrow strip of land that has water on both sides and joins two larger bodies of land called?

WHAT'S BEING TESTED?

Identify the type of question you are being asked.

Social studies tests often ask questions that involve reading comprehension. Other questions may require you to gather or interpret information from a map, graph, or chart. The following strategies will help you answer different kinds of questions.

Reading Comprehension Questions

What to do:

1. Determine the content and organization of the selection.

2. Analyze the questions.
Do they ask you to *recall facts?*

Do they ask you to *make judgments?*

3. Read the selection.

4. Answer the questions.

How to do it:

Read the **title.** Skim the selection. Look for key words that indicate time, cause-and-effect, or comparison.

Look for **key words** in the stem:
<u>According to</u> the selection . . .
The selection <u>states</u> that . . .

The <u>main idea</u> of the selection is . . .
The author <u>would likely</u> agree that . . .

Read quickly. Keep the questions in mind.

Try out each distractor and choose the best answer. Refer back to the selection if necessary.

Example:
A Region of Diversity The Khmer empire was one of many kingdoms in Southeast Asia. Unlike the Khmer empire, however, the other kingdoms were small because Southeast Asia's mountains kept people protected and apart. People had little contact with those who lived outside their own valley.

Why were most kingdoms in Southeast Asia small?
A disease killed many people
B lack of food
C climate was too hot
D mountains kept people apart

TIP▶ The key word <u>because</u> tells why the kingdoms were small.
(The correct answer is D.)

Map Questions

What to do:	How to do it:
1. Determine what kind of information is presented on the map.	Read the map **title.** It will indicate the purpose of the map. Study the **map key.** It will explain the symbols used on the map. Look at the **scale.** It will help you calculate distance between places on the map.
2. Read the question. Determine which component on the map will help you find the answer.	Look for **key words** in the stem. About <u>how far</u> . . . [use the scale] <u>What crops</u> were grown in . . . [use the map key]
3. Look at the map and answer the question in your own words.	Do not read the distractors yet.
4. Choose the best answer.	Decide which distractor agrees with the answer you determined from the map.

Eastern Europe: Language Groups

In which of these countries are Thraco-Illyrian languages spoken?

A Romania
B Albania
C Hungary
D Lithuania

TIP▶ Read the labels and the key to understand the map.
(The correct answer is B.)

Graph Questions

What to do:

1. Determine the purpose of the graph.

2. Determine what information on the graph will help you find the answer.

3. Choose the best answer.

How to do it:

Read the graph **title.** It indicates what the graph represents.

Read the **labels** on the graph or on the key. They tell the units of measurement used by the graph.

Decide which distractor agrees with the answer you determined from the graph.

Example

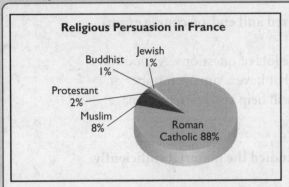

A **Circle graph** shows the relationship of parts to the whole in terms of percentages.

After Roman Catholics, the next largest religious population in France is
A Buddhist   **C** Jewish
B Protestant   **D** Muslim

TIP▶ Compare the percentages listed in the labels.
(The correct answer is D.)

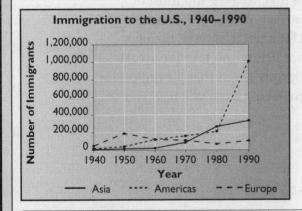

A **line graph** shows a pattern or change over time by the direction of the line.

Between 1980 and 1990, immigration to the U.S. from the Americas
A decreased a little   **C** stayed about the same
B increased greatly   **D** increased a little

TIP▶ Compare the vertical distance between the two
       correct points on the line graph.
(The correct answer is B.)

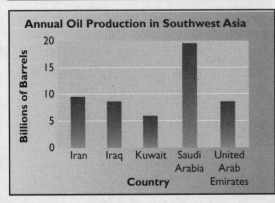

A **bar graph** compares differences in quantity by showing bars of different lengths.

Saudi Arabia produces about how many more billion of barrels of oil a year than Iran?
A 5 million   **C** 15 million
B 10 million   **D** 20 million

TIP▶ Compare the heights of the bars to find the
       difference.
(The correct answer is B.)

NOTE TO THE STUDENT

Test Prep Workbook for American Government contains multiple-choice test questions written specifically for Prentice Hall's *Magruder's American Government*. This booklet will help you prepare for American government tests in the following ways:

The test questions provide practice in answering multiple-choice questions.

You may need to practice answering multiple-choice questions. Even if you have studied for a test, you may sometimes choose incorrect answers. For example, you might read a question too quickly and not fully understand what the question is asking. Answering practice questions in this booklet will help you correctly answer more questions on the real test.

The test questions help you prepare for standardized and end-of-course exams.

Standardized and end-of-course exams usually have lots of questions. A good way to practice for these exams is to take practice tests that have a similar number of questions. Taking the practice tests in this booklet will help you learn to manage your time better on the actual exams.

The test questions help you make sure you have studied the material sufficiently.

Preparing for a test involves more than just taking a practice test. You must be able to recall the facts you have read and apply those facts on the test. Just taking a practice test is not a good substitute for studying for a test. However, taking a practice test can show you how well you have studied before you take the actual test. Finally, at the end of this booklet, you will find study sheets that list important details from each unit. Reviewing these sheets before taking a test will help you recall the facts that are likely to be on that test.

UNIT 1—FOUNDATIONS OF AMERICAN GOVERNMENT

Multiple Choice
Identify the letter of the choice that best completes the statement or answers the question.

MAIN IDEAS

_____ 1. Among the broad purposes of the United States government spelled out in the Preamble to the Constitution is the obligation to
   a. keep the executive and legislative branches of government separate.
   b. create an autocratic form of government.
   c. defend the country against Americans who oppose its policies.
   d. provide for justice and the people's general welfare.

_____ 2. The theory underlying modern democracies was developed to challenge the idea that
   a. those of royal birth have absolute authority to rule.
   b. the people as a whole are the sole source of political power.
   c. the head of a family, clan, or tribe has the natural right to govern.
   d. the strongest person or group has the right to control others by force.

_____ 3. The dominant political unit in the world today is the
   a. government.   c. Constitution.
   b. nation.   d. state.

_____ 4. A federal government is one in which
   a. all power is concentrated in the central government.
   b. limited powers are assigned to a central agency by independent states.
   c. power is divided between a central government and local governments.
   d. powers are divided between a legislative branch and an executive branch.

_____ 5. Which of the following statements is NOT true of parliamentary government?
   a. The executive is chosen by the legislature.
   b. The legislature is subject to the direct control of the executive.
   c. The prime minister and cabinet are part of the legislative branch.
   d. The prime minister and cabinet must resign if they lose the support of a majority of the legislature.

_____ 6. The individual 50 States lack which basic characteristic of a state?
   a. government   c. Constitution
   b. sovereignty   d. defined population

_____ 7. Which of the following statements about sovereign states is NOT true?
    a. Sovereign states decide their own foreign and domestic policies.
    b. Sovereign states can determine their own form of government.
    c. A county or city is considered sovereign because it is subordinate to a larger form of government.
    d. Sovereign states have supreme power within their own territories.

_____ 8. All political powers in a state are concentrated at the central level under which form of government?
    a. federal   c. unitary
    b. confederate   d. executive

_____ 9. Which of the following is among the purposes of government outlined in the Preamble to the Constitution?
    a. defending the nation against foreign enemies
    b. insuring order and domestic tranquility
    c. promoting the general welfare of the citizens
    d. all of the above

_____ 10. Which statement about the social contract theory is NOT true?
    a. The state was created voluntarily by a free people.
    b. The state is a natural extension of people's family structure.
    c. Governmental powers are granted by the people.
    d. Governmental powers may be limited by the people.

_____ 11. Which of the following illustrates the concept of equality of opportunity?
    a. Public schools may not exclude students because of their sex or race.
    b. Citizens must obey the tax laws but may work to change them.
    c. Government may limit the beliefs and ideas of individuals.
    d. Senators consider testimony both for and against Supreme Court nominees.

_____ 12. In the charter colonies, most governmental matters were handled by
    a. the British monarch.   c. a proprietor.
    b. Parliament.   d. the colonists.

_____ 13. All of the following influenced the Framers in developing the Constitution EXCEPT
    a. State constitutions.
    b. John Locke's *Two Treatises of Government.*
    c. Virginia's royal charter.
    d. British tradition.

_____ 14. Which feature did the State constitutions and the Articles of Confederation have in common?
  a. royal governors
  b. bill of rights
  c. principle of popular sovereignty
  d. a strong executive elected by popular vote

_____ 15. Which of these State constitutions is the oldest and still in force today?
  a. Massachusetts
  b. South Carolina
  c. New Hampshire
  d. Virginia

_____ 16. After the Revolutionary War, the National Government
  a. proved too weak to deal with growing economic and political problems.
  b. refused to repay the war debt it owed to the States.
  c. permitted the States to make agreements with foreign governments.
  d. began imposing harsh tax policies on property owners and merchants.

_____ 17. Which of the following statements about the inauguration of George Washington as the first U.S. president is NOT true?
  a. It followed his unanimous election in the Electoral College.
  b. It took place in New York City, the country's temporary capital.
  c. It came after the ratification of the Constitution.
  d. It followed Washington's appointment of James Madison as the first Vice President.

_____ 18. The government set up by the Articles of Confederation had
  a. no legislative or judicial branch.
  b. only a legislative and an executive branch.
  c. only a legislative branch, consisting of a unicameral Congress.
  d. only a legislative branch, consisting of a bicameral Congress.

_____ 19. Which was an achievement of the Second Continental Congress?
  a. preparing a Declaration of Rights
  b. raising an American army
  c. establishing a strong central government
  d. passing the Intolerable Acts

_____ 20. Parliament first limited the power of the Crown under the
  a. Intolerable Acts.
  b. Petition of Right.
  c. Stamp Act of 1765.
  d. English Bill of Rights.

_____ 21. *The Federalist* was written to
   a. win support for the Constitution in New York.
   b. expose the lack of civil liberties protected in the Constitution.
   c. urge ratification of the Constitution in Virginia.
   d. condemn the Constitution for the absence of any mention of God.

_____ 22. Which of the following directly influenced the Framers in the development of the Constitution?
   a. Chinese tradition
   b. the Articles of Confederation
   c. Spanish tradition
   d. Virginia's royal charter

_____ 23. By the mid-1700s, British rule in the colonies was marked by
   a. allowing a certain degree of self-rule to the colonists.
   b. imposing harsh and restrictive trade practices.
   c. passing increasingly high taxes.
   d. forcing the colonies to attack other colonial powers.

_____ 24. Delegates met at Mount Vernon and Annapolis to
   a. recommend a federal plan for regulating commerce.
   b. recommend a way to start a national army.
   c. recommend ways to end slavery.
   d. attend a social gathering in honor of George Washington.

_____ 25. The first State constitutions, adopted after independence,
   a. placed most authority with the State governors.
   b. provided for lengthy terms for elective offices.
   c. placed most authority with the State legislatures.
   d. extended voting rights to all adult State residents.

_____ 26. Much of the work of the Framers centered around the proposals that had been set out in
   a. the Virginia Plan.
   b. the New Jersey Plan.
   c. *The Federalist.*
   d. the Declaration of Independence.

_____ 27. The success of which plan led to the Constitutional Convention of 1787?
   a. Albany Plan of Union
   b. Second Continental Congress's "plan of confederation"
   c. interstate plan for regulating trade between Virginia and Maryland
   d. compromise reached between the Virginia and New Jersey plans

_____ 28. The idea that the people have the right to abolish an abusive and unresponsive government was FIRST formally expressed by Americans in the
   a. Constitution.
   b. Petition of Right.
   c. Declaration of Rights.
   d. Declaration of Independence.

____ 29. With the words, "We the People," the Constitution establishes its authority on the basis of
    a. popular sovereignty.
    b. the rule of law.
    c. the separation of powers.
    d. limited government.

____ 30. The President's Cabinet is an example of informal amendment by
    a. unwritten custom.
    b. court decision.
    c. State action.
    d. basic legislation.

____ 31. In most cases involving judicial review, the courts have
    a. had their decisions overturned by Congress.
    b. found the governmental actions in question to be unconstitutional.
    c. found the governmental actions in question to be constitutional.
    d. had their decisions vetoed by the President.

____ 32. Which of the following is a method of formal amendment?
    a. proposal by three-fourths of the House of Representatives and ratification by conventions in three-fourths of State legislatures
    b. proposal by two-thirds of the Senate and ratification by two-thirds of State legislatures
    c. proposal by two-thirds of Congress and ratification by three-fourths of State legislatures
    d. all of the above

____ 33. The basic constitutional rights of the people were FIRST set out in the
    a. 13th, 14th, and 15th amendments.
    b. 10th Amendment.
    c. Bill of Rights.
    d. Equal Rights Amendment.

____ 34. The legislative branch can check the judicial branch by its power to
    a. name federal judges.
    b. remove judges through impeachment.
    c. declare executive actions unconstitutional.
    d. override a presidential veto.

____ 35. The President's power to veto an act of Congress is an example of
    a. executive agreement.
    b. judicial review.
    c. checks and balances.
    d. limited government.

____ 36. Which of the following accounts for the ability of the Constitution to endure for more than 200 years?
    a. built-in provisions for accommodating change
    b. detailed provisions that anticipated changing customs
    c. very specific language that limits reinterpretation
    d. inflexible provisions designed to resist change

_____ 37. According to Article V of the Constitution, no amendment may
    a. deprive a State of its equal representation in the Senate.
    b. abolish the protections guaranteed in the Bill of Rights.
    c. deny people the right to vote because of race, color, or gender.
    d. reestablish slavery or other forms of involuntary servitude.

_____ 38. Which of the following is mentioned by the Constitution and its amendments?
    a. succession of Vice President to presidency
    b. political parties
    c. custom of senatorial courtesy
    d. the President's Cabinet

_____ 39. Which of the following is NOT an example of the checks and balances system?
    a. The President makes an executive agreement.
    b. The Supreme Court declares a law passed by Congress to be unconstitutional.
    c. The President vetoes a bill.
    d. The Senate approves the President's nominee for Supreme Court justice.

_____ 40. Which of the following was formally amended to the Constitution?
    a. equality of rights for women   c. prohibition of child labor
    b. prohibition of alcoholic beverages   d. balanced federal budget

_____ 41. The system of federalism provides for all of the following EXCEPT
    a. local action in matters of local concern.
    b. a dual system of government.
    c. uniform laws among the States.
    d. strength through unity.

_____ 42. Concurrent powers are those that are
    a. exercised simultaneously by the National and the State governments.
    b. exercised by State governments alone.
    c. exercised by the National Government alone.
    d. denied to both the National and the State governments.

_____ 43. States must honor the legality of one another's civil laws because of the
    a. Necessary and Proper Clause.   c. Supremacy Clause.
    b. Full Faith and Credit Clause.   d. Interstate Compacts Clause.

_____ 44. Which of the following is an expressed power of the National Government?
    a. the power to coin money   c. the power to acquire territory
    b. the power to license doctors   d. the power to grant divorces

_____ 45. Citizens who commit a crime in one State and then flee to another State to escape prosecution are to be returned to the original State under
    a.   the Full Faith and Credit Clause.
    b.   the Privileges and Immunities Clause.
    c.   extradition.
    d.   any interstate compact involving all 50 States.

_____ 46. The Constitution requires the National Government to guarantee
    a.   block grants to every State.
    b.   schools for every community.
    c.   an equal number of representatives for every State.
    d.   a republican form of government for every State.

_____ 47. Which of the following is NOT among the obligations that the National Government has to the States?
    a.   protection against foreign attack and domestic violence
    b.   guarantee of a representative form of government
    c.   recognition of each State's legal existence and physical boundaries
    d.   recognition of State constitutions as the supreme law of the land

_____ 48. Agreements States enter into with both foreign nations and other States with the consent of Congress are
    a.   interstate compacts.   c.   extraditions.
    b.   acts of admission.   d.   enabling acts.

_____ 49. Which of the following is the basic characteristic of federalism?
    a.   It divides power between a National Government and State governments.
    b.   It gives most power to the National Government.
    c.   It gives most power to local units of government.
    d.   It encourages citizen participation in government.

_____ 50. Which statement about local government is accurate?
    a.   Local government has no relationship with State governments.
    b.   Local government is an extension of the federal government.
    c.   Local government is a subunit of State government.
    d.   Local government supercedes the authority of State government.

UNIT 2—POLITICAL BEHAVIOR

Multiple Choice
Identify the letter of the choice that best completes the statement or answers the question.

MAIN IDEAS

_____ 1. In the United States, a political party is made up of a group of people who
    a.   disagree on how to resolve the basic issues affecting the country.
    b.   work to get candidates elected to political offices.
    c.   work separately to support one major program or policy.
    d.   support split-ticket voting.

_____ 2. A multi-party system
    a.   tends to produce a stable government.
    b.   helps one party win the support of a majority of voters.
    c.   is composed of parties with special interests.
    d.   promotes the ideological consensus of the public.

_____ 3. Which statement does NOT describe one type of minor party?
    a.   The members of a minor party are united by a particular group of viewpoints.
    b.   A minor party is a party that has broken away from a major party.
    c.   The members of a minor party tend to support the platform of a major party.
    d.   A minor party expresses discontent over the state of the economy.

_____ 4. People belong to a particular political party
    a.   according to regulations of State law.
    b.   voluntarily, because they made a personal choice.
    c.   based on the location of the State in which they live.
    d.   according to regulations of federal law.

_____ 5. Which of the following statements about Federalists is TRUE?
    a.   They called for a strict interpretation of the Constitution.
    b.   George Washington founded their party.
    c.   They were generally supported by farmers.
    d.   A strong national government was of great concern to them.

_____ 6. Which of the following is NOT a major function of either of the two major parties in the United States?
    a.   To keep the general public informed about key issues.
    b.   To monitor the conduct of its candidates in office.
    c.   To assure the qualifications of candidates for office.
    d.   To unite people and concentrate solely on one public policy matter.

_____ 7. Over time, the ideas first developed by minor parties are often _____ by major parties.
    a. ignored
    b. borrowed
    c. suppressed
    d. attacked

_____ 8. Parties that hold a particular set of beliefs and have often supported Marxist thinking are known as
    a. ideological parties.
    b. single-issue parties.
    c. splinter parties.
    d. economic protest parties.

_____ 9. Membership in either of the two major parties is
    a. closely regulated by federal law.
    b. closely regulated by State law.
    c. based on economic status.
    d. based on personal choice.

_____ 10. The two-party system developed in the United States mainly because
    a. the Constitution established a democratic government.
    b. conflicts about the Constitution created opposing viewpoints.
    c. leaders and voters agreed on the existence of two parties.
    d. it was voted on and approved by both houses of Congress.

_____ 11. The era of one-party domination that began in 1968 was different from past eras of one-party domination because
    a. the Republican party gained no new members in Congress.
    b. the Democratic party gained no new members in Congress.
    c. one party controlled Congress while the other controlled the presidency.
    d. minor parties interfered with the power of the Republican party.

_____ 12. Minor parties have contributed MOST to United States politics by
    a. causing major parties to adopt their ideas.
    b. providing more candidates from which voters can choose.
    c. placing their presidential candidates on the ballot.
    d. establishing political precedents.

_____ 13. The functions of the major parties in United States politics include
    a. nominating candidates for office.
    b. insuring the good performance of their elected candidates.
    c. providing a mechanism for the conduct of government.
    d. all of the above.

_____ 14. Which of the following groups has tended to support the Democratic party in recent decades?
    a. the business community
    b. Protestants
    c. union members
    d. white males

_____ 15. The two major parties have members who take all of the following roles EXCEPT
   a.   party leaders.   c.   party independents.
   b.   loyal party members and voters.   d.   party officeholders.

_____ 16. Which of the following is NOT a long-term trend marking the expansion of suffrage in the United States?
   a.   removing restrictive requirements based on religious belief
   b.   the Federal Government taking less of a role in protecting suffrage rights
   c.   eliminating requirements based on race
   d.   eliminating requirements based on tax payments

_____ 17. The provisions of the Voting Rights Act of 1965 and its amendments of 1970, 1975, and 1982 apply to
   a.   all national, State, and local elections.
   b.   federal elections only.
   c.   State and local elections only.
   d.   all federal and State elections, but not to all local elections.

_____ 18. The term *political socialization* can be defined as the
   a.   process in which individual initiative is abandoned in favor of party politics.
   b.   belief that one's vote does not count.
   c.   process by which people formulate their political attitudes and opinions.
   d.   practice of voting for candidates of only one specific party in any given election.

_____ 19. Literacy tests worked to deny the right to vote to African Americans primarily because
   a.   all white voters had higher literacy rates.
   b.   the tests were only required in Southern States.
   c.   African Americans were asked questions that were more difficult than those asked of prospective white voters.
   d.   it was specifically provided for in the Constitution.

_____ 20. Which act first established a federal commission to investigate claims of individual voter discrimination?
   a.   Civil Rights Act of 1957   c.   Civil Rights Act of 1964
   b.   Civil Rights Act of 1960   d.   Voting Rights Act of 1965

_____ 21. Today many States require that all voters
   a.   be citizens of the United States and residents of the State.
   b.   meet specific literacy requirements.
   c.   be familiar with the candidates and issues before voting.
   d.   be natural-born citizens of the United States.

10

_____ 22. A person who votes in the presidential election but does not vote for a congressional candidate in the same election is known as
   a. a "cannot-voter."   c. an independent voter.
   b. a "nonvoting voter."   d. an actual nonvoter.

_____ 23. The single most significant predictor of a person's partisan voting behavior is his or her
   a. party identification.   c. political efficacy.
   b. educational background.   d. perceptions of government.

_____ 24. The 15th Amendment, ratified in 1870, did not secure the right of African Americans to vote primarily because
   a. it did not state that voting rights could not be denied to African Americans.
   b. the Federal Government did not intervene to uphold the amendment.
   c. it was repealed by Congress shortly after ratification.
   d. it prevented State leaders from acting on behalf of potential voters who were being discriminated against.

_____ 25. Gerrymandering is unfair because
   a. no one has the right to divide electoral districts for elections.
   b. it sets district boundaries to decrease one group's voting strength.
   c. it makes voter registration difficult for uneducated white males.
   d. it increases the voting power of minority groups.

_____ 26. The nominating stage is important in the electoral process mostly because
   a. only Republicans and Democrats can take part in nominations.
   b. nominations set real limits to the choices voters can make in general elections.
   c. major party candidates exert more effort to win nominations than elections.
   d. in a democracy the general election is little more than a formality.

_____ 27. Why are voting machines used?
   a. to eliminate the election process
   b. to increase the number of persons needed to administer elections
   c. to minimize vote-counting errors
   d. to encourage manual vote counting

_____ 28. Voters are asked to complete election ballots in all of the following ways EXCEPT
   a. moving levers on a voting machine.   c. returning a mail-in ballot.
   b. marking a punch card.   d. raising hands at a public meeting.

_____ 29. Campaign contributions to a presidential candidate can
   a. come from any foreign country.   c. all be made anonymously.
   b. be for any amount of money.   d. be made by any American.

_____ 30. The oldest form of the nominating process in the United States is
   a. the convention.
   b. a congressional caucus.
   c. the direct primary.
   d. self-announcement.

_____ 31. The most costly items in a typical campaign budget today are
   a. newspaper and magazine advertisements.
   b. pamphlets and posters.
   c. travel and entertainment.
   d. television advertisements.

_____ 32. Which of the following statements about PACs is FALSE?
   a. They can raise funds only for presidential and congressional campaigns.
   b. They distribute money to those candidates who are sympathetic to their policy goals.
   c. They can give no more than $5,000 to any one federal candidate in an election.
   d. They can give no more than $15,000 a year to a political party.

_____ 33. The smallest geographic unit for conducting an election is a
   a. precinct.
   b. polling place.
   c. county.
   d. ballot.

_____ 34. Which of the following ballots tends to encourage straight-ticket voting?
   a. office-group ballot
   b. party-column ballot
   c. nonpartisan ballot
   d. "bed-sheet" ballot

_____ 35. All of the following are loopholes in the current federal election laws EXCEPT
   a. the use of soft money for "party building" activities.
   b. money spent by an independent person or group on behalf of a candidate.
   c. the prominent use of issue ads.
   d. unlimited contributions by PACs to any one federal candidate.

_____ 36. Which of the following is the earliest and one of the most significant agents in the political socialization process?
   a. family
   b. place of residence
   c. group affiliation
   d. gender

_____ 37. The impact of the mass media on the public agenda can best be described as its ability to
   a. tell people whom to vote for.
   b. focus the public's attention on specific issues.
   c. tell people what opinions to have about those issues.
   d. focus the public's attention on how to vote.

____ 38. Attitudes held by a significant number of people concerning governmental and political
questions are known as
a. the mass media.
b. public opinion.
c. interest groups.
d. public policies.

____ 39. "Universe" is a term used to describe
a. a politician's constituency.
b. the entire group of persons sampled in a given poll.
c. the entire group of persons whose opinions a poll seeks to measure.
d. the group that supports the activities of an interest group.

____ 40. Public opinion is made known through all of the following EXCEPT
a. interest groups.
b. personal contacts.
c. the media.
d. peer groups.

____ 41. What would be your BEST advice to a person who wants to learn more about political issues?
a. Watch only television news and commentary shows daily.
b. Pay attention only to newspaper stories.
c. Explore a variety of sources of political information.
d. Regularly read the major newspapers and news magazines.

____ 42. The term "public opinion" is misleading because
a. opinions have no place in politics or government.
b. Americans belong to many different publics, each with a distinctive viewpoint.
c. most Americans consider political opinions to be a private matter.
d. no two people in the public really agree on any issue.

____ 43. The best example of the use of random sampling to determine who will be elected as your
school president would involve
a. asking each student in your class whom he or she would vote for.
b. asking one student in each classroom whom he or she would vote for.
c. picking out a specific number of students as they leave the school, and asking whom they
would vote for.
d. asking every seventh student on an alphabetized list of all students whom they would
vote for.

____ 44. Which of the following steps in scientific polling comes FIRST?
a. tabulating the data
b. constructing the sample
c. preparing valid questions
d. defining the universe

____ 45. All of the following are examples of groups that promote causes EXCEPT the
a. American Civil Liberties Union.
b. American Legion.
c. National Rifle Association.
d. Sierra Club.

_____ 46. A labor union is an organization of workers who
    a. hold exactly the same political beliefs.
    b. represent the interests of the business community.
    c. work in the same job or industry.
    d. work on farms.

_____ 47. The term *grass roots* refers to
    a. trade associations.   c. average voters.
    b. party politicians.   d. interest groups.

_____ 48. A positive aspect of interest groups is that they
    a. help stimulate interest in public affairs.
    b. eliminate the need for factions in government.
    c. use propaganda to influence public policy.
    d. have a strong influence on political parties.

_____ 49. All of the following are propaganda techniques EXCEPT
    a. presenting only one side of an issue.
    b. using glittering generalities.
    c. supporting a government policy change.
    d. the bandwagon approach.

_____ 50. One way interest groups become involved in the election process is by
    a. providing campaign funds.
    b. changing into a labor union.
    c. having members secretly join political parties.
    d. nominating candidates for office.

UNIT 3—THE LEGISLATIVE BRANCH

Multiple Choice
Identify the letter of the choice that best completes the statement or answers the question.

MAIN IDEAS

_____ 1. The lawmaking function of Congress is central to democracy because
   a. it enables elected representatives to do the daily work of government.
   b. legislative powers are necessary to check the power of the President.
   c. it frees members of Congress from the pressures of public opinion.
   d. it is the means by which the public will becomes public policy.

_____ 2. Which statement about the Senate is true?
   a. It has two members from each State.
   b. Its members are chosen by State legislatures.
   c. Each member represents one congressional district.
   d. Seats are apportioned among the States according to their populations.

_____ 3. Which fact disqualifies a person from representing Utah in the Senate?
   a. The candidate was born in Guatemala.
   b. The candidate is 43 years old.
   c. The candidate lives in Utah but works in Idaho.
   d. The candidate has been a citizen for eight years.

_____ 4. The regular period of time during which Congress conducts its business is called a
   a. prorogue.   c. special session.
   b. session.   d. term.

_____ 5. The House may refuse to seat a member-elect only if he or she
   a. has engaged in disorderly behavior.
   b. has violated the code of ethics passed by the House in 1977.
   c. does not meet constitutional standards of age, citizenship, and residency.
   d. does not meet informal standards set by two-thirds of the members.

_____ 6. The number of Senate seats held by each State is
   a. set by the Census Bureau.
   b. based on State populations.
   c. the same as the number of House seats.
   d. fixed by the Constitution.

____ 7. The Framers of the Constitution favored bicameralism because
    a. two houses could block the acts of a single President.
    b. it allowed for fair and equal representation of the States at the national level.
    c. Great Britain had only one house of Parliament.
    d. one house would spend more money than two.

____ 8. Which of the following is true of the House of Representatives?
    a. It currently has 100 members.
    b. The total number of seats in the House is fixed by the Constitution.
    c. The number of terms a representative may serve is fixed by the Constitution.
    d. Every State is represented by at least one member.

____ 9. On the average, which group of people occupy the majority of seats in Congress?
    a. African Americans   c. women
    b. white, middle-aged men   d. Asian Americans

____ 10. Senators are elected to serve
    a. two-year terms.   c. four-year terms.
    b. three-year terms.   d. six-year terms.

____ 11. Why does the Constitution guarantee that the courts may not prosecute members of Congress for what they say in the House or Senate in relation to congressional business?
    a. Members never criticize one another.
    b. Freedom of speech is a vital part of legislative debate.
    c. The courts have no jurisdiction in Washington, D.C.
    d. Members have the same privileges in their districts.

____ 12. The powers of Congress are affected by all of the following EXCEPT what the
    a. Constitution expressly says Congress may do.
    b. Constitution says only the States may do.
    c. States' constitutions say Congress may do.
    d. Constitution is silent about.

____ 13. The Supreme Court ruling in *Gibbons* v. *Ogden* expanded the
    a. currency power by including paper money as legal tender.
    b. power to tax by allowing a tax on incomes.
    c. commerce power to include all commercial interactions.
    d. power over territories to include the taking of private property.

____ 14. According to the Constitution, who has the sole power to impeach the President?
    a. The House of Representatives   c. the Supreme Court
    b. the Vice President   d. State courts

____ 15. Which of the following is an example of the investigatory powers of Congress?
    a. accepting a treaty made by the President
    b. the power to regulate commerce with foreign nations
    c. the power to lay and collect taxes
    d. gathering information useful in making legislative decisions

____ 16. All the following expressed powers belong to Congress EXCEPT
    a. the power to declare war.   c. the power to naturalize citizens.
    b. the power to tax exports.   d. the power to raise an army.

____ 17. Under the Constitution, Congress has the sole power to
    a. act as the commander in chief.   c. declare war.
    b. meet with foreign leaders.   d. none of the above.

____ 18. All treaties must be approved by a two-thirds vote of
    a. the Senate.   c. both houses of Congress.
    b. the House.   d. the Supreme Court.

____ 19. Why did the Framers include the Necessary and Proper Clause in the Constitution?
    a. to empower Congress to pass laws needed to carry out the expressed powers
    b. to limit congressional powers to those expressly stated in the Constitution
    c. to define the scope of the inherent powers of Congress
    d. to set forth those powers considered necessary to the States

____ 20. All the following are implied powers of Congress EXCEPT the power to
    a. set maximum work hours.   c. fund education programs.
    b. restrict arms sales.   d. censor radio and TV programs.

____ 21. Who has the power to propose Constitutional amendments?
    a. the President   c. Congress
    b. the Supreme Court   d. State courts

____ 22. The implied powers doctrine, upheld in *McCulloch* v. *Maryland*, gives Congress the power to do
    a. only what the Supreme Court authorizes it to do.
    b. only what is absolutely necessary to carry out the expressed powers.
    c. anything reasonably related to carrying out the expressed powers.
    d. anything it decides is in the public interest.

____ 23. The main reason that Congress creates committees is to
    a. divide the workload.   c. introduce new bills.
    b. educate new members.   d. create party power bases.

____ 24. Which of the following is a way a bill can become a law without the President's signature?
  a. The President delegates the signing of a bill to the Vice President.
  b. The President waits until the Congress is not in session.
  c. The President fails to act on the bill within 10 days of receiving it while Congress is in session.
  d. The President leaves the country.

____ 25. How and when bills reach the floor of the House is decided by the
  a. Ways and Means Committee.
  c. Appropriations Committee.
  b. Rules Committee.
  d. Judiciary Committee.

____ 26. Bills are introduced in the Senate by
  a. the Rules Committee.
  c. investigative committees.
  b. individual senators.
  d. the majority floor leader.

____ 27. The House Rules Committee may do all of the following EXCEPT
  a. set conditions for considering a bill.
  c. prevent consideration of a bill.
  b. speed up consideration of a bill.
  d. attach amendments to a bill.

____ 28. The main way to end a filibuster is by
  a. a two-thirds vote of the Senate.
  c. convening a conference committee.
  b. invoking the Cloture Rule.
  d. voting the filibusterer out of office.

____ 29. Majority floor leaders hold considerable power due mainly to the fact that
  a. they are the most popular leaders.
  b. presiding officers choose them.
  c. the majority party has more seats than the other party has.
  d. they are assisted by a powerful whip.

____ 30. The role of the House Rules Committee is played in the Senate by the
  a. president *pro tempore*.
  c. whip.
  b. president of the Senate.
  d. majority floor leader.

____ 31. In 1997, 26-year-old Representative Harold Ford Jr. became a member of the 105th Congress. What happened the year before this that made his election possible?
  a. Congress passed the Voter Registration Act of 1997.
  b. Congress lowered the age of a member of the House to 26.
  c. He had lived in the state of Tennessee for at least seven years.
  d. He celebrated his twenty-fifth birthday.

_____ 32. Why is a senator's term in office different in length than that of a representative's?
   a. Senators' terms are shorter because they require less experience than representatives do.
   b. Senators' terms are longer so they can be staggered; therefore, a majority of senators is always experienced.
   c. Senators' terms are limited to only one term in office; therefore their term in office is longer.
   d. Senators' terms are shorter in order to make sure they accurately represent their constituents.

_____ 33. Congress shares powers with the President in the field of foreign affairs. What other powers do Congress and the President share?
   a. judicial powers
   b. postal powers
   c. territorial powers
   d. war powers

_____ 34. What is the implied power expressed by the Necessary and Proper Clause in the Constitution?
   a. Congress's ability to make laws is severely limited by the Constitution.
   b. Congress is given limited authority to interpret reserved powers.
   c. Congress must follow a concrete interpretation of the Constitution.
   d. Congress can make any law that it deems appropriate.

_____ 35. What nonlegislative action has the Senate performed only during the presidencies of Andrew Johnson and Bill Clinton?
   a. voted to acquit
   b. voted to impeach
   c. withdrew deficit financing
   d. declared bankruptcy

_____ 36. The Constitution makes no mention of them, yet these bodies play an essential role in the lawmaking process. Their job is to sift through and decide the fate of bills. What are they?
   a. quorums
   b. committees of the whole
   c. standing committees
   d. conference committees

_____ 37. The purpose of a filibuster is to
   a. invoke the rule of cloture.
   b. overrule a Presidential veto.
   c. allow quorum calls.
   d. prevent action on a bill.

_____ 38. strict constructionist: _____ ; liberal constructionist: Alexander Hamilton
   a. James Madison
   b. John Adams
   c. Thomas Jefferson
   d. George Washington

_____ 39. What event brought *McCulloch* v. *Maryland* before the Supreme Court?
   a.   The state of Maryland based its congressional districts on race.
   b.   The state of Maryland attempted to tax federal bank notes.
   c.   The state of Maryland governor disagreed with the power of Congress to regulate interstate commerce.
   d.   The state of Maryland refused to follow the federal standards of weights and measures.

_____ 40. Which of the following determines who holds the position of Speaker of the House?
   a.   the President   c.   the Senate
   b.   the House   d.   the joint houses of Congress

UNIT 4—THE EXECUTIVE BRANCH

Multiple Choice
Identify the letter of the choice that best completes the statement or answers the question.

MAIN IDEAS

_____ 1. According to the Constitution, the President must
  a. be a man who owns property.
  b. be at least 35 years of age.
  c. have held one major public office.
  d. have lived in the U. S. for at least 20 years.

_____ 2. The electoral system broke down in the election of 1800 because of the
  a. rise of political parties.
  b. 12th Amendment.
  c. use of the national convention as a nominating device.
  d. appearance of a presidential primary.

_____ 3. A President can serve no more than _____ years in office.
  a. 8   c. 10
  b. 4   d. 12

_____ 4. According to the Presidential Succession Act of 1947, which of these officers follows the Vice President in the line of presidential succession?
  a. Speaker of the House   c. president *pro tempore* of the Senate
  b. secretary of state   d. secretary of the treasury

_____ 5. The President may decide to resume duties after an illness by informing Congress that no inability exists, but that decision can be challenged by
  a. Congress.
  b. the Vice President.
  c. the Vice President and a majority of the Cabinet.
  d. any representative in the House of Representatives.

_____ 6. The national convention is held to accomplish all of the following EXCEPT
  a. unify the party behind its candidates.
  b. pick its presidential candidate.
  c. select the party's delegates.
  d. adopt the party's platform.

_____ 7. Which of the following statements is NOT an argument against the electoral college system?
    a. A candidate who loses the popular vote may still be elected President.
    b. An elector may vote for someone other than the voter-selected candidate.
    c. A strong third-party effort might throw the election into the House.
    d. The results depend upon how State congressional districts are drawn.

_____ 8. A presidential primary can be
    a. a process to select delegates to the convention.
    b. an election to determine voters' choice among candidates.
    c. both of the above.
    d. none of the above.

_____ 9. The first and most widely publicized caucus today is held in the State of
    a. California.   c. New Hampshire.
    b. New Jersey.   d. Iowa.

_____ 10. The Framers of the Constitution called for the President to be elected by
    a. Congress.   c. a body of electors.
    b. a direct vote of the people.   d. the State legislatures.

_____ 11. The power of the presidency has been cause for debate MAINLY because
    a. the presidency is the most powerful office in the world.
    b. the Constitution provided a loose definition of executive power.
    c. the presidency is an office that operates in full view of the public.
    d. leaders wanted to prevent the President from becoming a tyrant.

_____ 12. Which of the following statements about the President's power of removal is TRUE?
    a. For those offices for which Senate approval is required for appointment, Senate consent is also required for removal.
    b. Any person holding office by presidential appointment with Senate consent must remain in that office until the Senate confirms a successor.
    c. Any person holding office by presidential appointment with Senate consent may be removed only for incompetence.
    d. As a general rule, the President may remove any officeholders he or she has appointed.

_____ 13. The President CANNOT exercise judicial power by
    a. granting amnesty to a group of law violators.
    b. reducing the length of a sentence.
    c. granting pardons in cases of impeachment.
    d. postponing the carrying out of a sentence.

_____ 14. The debate over the powers of the presidency is essentially a debate
    a. about Article III of the Constitution.
    b. between supporters of a strong presidency and supporters of a weak presidency.
    c. about the system of checks and balances.
    d. about the electoral college system.

_____ 15. The difference between a treaty and an executive agreement is that
    a. a treaty is with a foreign state but an executive agreement is domestic.
    b. a treaty must begin in the Senate but an executive agreement is made wholly by the President.
    c. the President needs Senate approval for a treaty but not for an executive agreement.
    d. a treaty ends or prevents a war but an executive agreement does not.

_____ 16. The President's power to execute the law covers
    a. all federal laws, whether or not the President agrees with them.
    b. only those federal laws that the President supports.
    c. only those laws that are described or implied in the Constitution.
    d. all the laws of foreign countries to which the United States sends aid.

_____ 17. When President Andrew Johnson fired his secretary of war in 1867, he was following
    a. Congress's orders.
    b. a strict construction of the Constitution.
    c. senatorial courtesy.
    d. the unwritten rule that the President may remove whomever he appoints.

_____ 18. A President can use armed forces abroad
    a. once Congress has approved the decision.
    b. after a declaration of war has been issued by Congress.
    c. pending approval by Congress within 48 hours.
    d. at his or her own discretion.

_____ 19. The President's power to grant pardons
    a. may be overridden by the Senate.
    b. applies to cases involving federal and State offenses.
    c. may be used in cases of impeachment.
    d. can be used before a person is charged with a crime.

_____ 20. The Federal Government is considered a bureaucracy primarily because it
    a. was established according to the practice and traditions set by past Presidents as they fulfilled their executive functions.
    b. consists of many agencies that do not function very efficiently in the performance of their duties.
    c. is a complex system of organization based on certain principles.
    d. is headed by the President, who represents the main bureau, or office.

_____ 21. Which one of the following is an example of an independent agency?
   a. Department of State
   b. National Aeronautics and Space Administration
   c. National Security Council
   d. Office of Management and Budget

_____ 22. The civil service system was finally established because of
   a. President Washington's actions creating the tradition.
   b. President Jefferson's support of political acceptability.
   c. President Jackson's development of the spoils system.
   d. President Garfield's assassination by an angry office seeker.

_____ 23. Which of the following was one of the original executive departments set up by Congress in 1789?
   a. Department of Justice   c. Department of Agriculture
   b. Department of Treasury   d. Department of Education

_____ 24. Which of the following are functions of employees working in the White House Office?
   a. advise the President on foreign, domestic, and defense matters
   b. preside over certain congressional hearings and legislative matters
   c. report to the President on the purchase of supplies for the government
   d. prosecute those accused of spying and treason against the government

_____ 25. The spoils system is
   a. the practice of hiring the most qualified candidates for federal jobs.
   b. the practice of giving offices and other favors of government to friends and supporters.
   c. completely unrelated to the practice of patronage.
   d. a democratic means of filling offices.

_____ 26. Which of the following are among the criteria for a President when choosing a Cabinet member?
   a. political party affiliation
   b. role in presidential election campaign
   c. qualifications and experience
   d. all of the above

_____ 27. The MAIN purpose of the National Security Council is to
   a. advise the President on all domestic, foreign, and military aspects of the nation's security.
   b. carry out secret operations in other countries to further the nation's security.
   c. provide support staff for the work of agencies like the FBI.
   d. report on security threats made against the White House.

_____ 28. Which one of the following agencies is a part of the Executive Office of the President?
    a. Social Security Administration
    b. Office of Management and Budget
    c. Federal Deposit Insurance Corporation
    d. Nuclear Regulatory Commission

_____ 29. The largest source of federal revenue from taxes comes from
    a. income taxes.   c. estate taxes.
    b. excise taxes.   d. custom duties.

_____ 30. One reason for the importance of the federal budget is that it
    a. determines how Social Security will be distributed.
    b. demonstrates Congress's stand on significant issues.
    c. determines which public programs will have money to operate.
    d. limits the sources from which budget money can come.

_____ 31. Which of the following limits on the Federal Government's power to tax is implied but not stated in the Constitution?
    a. No tax shall be levied on articles exported from any State.
    b. All taxes must be used for public purposes, not private purposes.
    c. States shall not be taxed for their governmental activities.
    d. States shall pay direct taxes proportionately based on population.

_____ 32. Although only Congress can appropriate the money that the Federal Government uses to operate, it is the _____ who initiate(s) the spending process.
    a. President   c. Budget Committee
    b. Supreme Court   d. voters

_____ 33. Public debt today is measured in _____ of dollars.
    a. thousands   c. billions
    b. millions   d. trillions

_____ 34. The process of preparing the federal budget begins with
    a. estimates from all agencies detailing yearly spending projections.
    b. plans for spending determined by the President.
    c. suggestions on spending from congressional committees.
    d. spending plans submitted by the Office of Management and Budget.

_____ 35. In recent decades, the Federal Government borrowed money mostly to
    a. finance special expensive projects.
    b. provide funds for crisis situations, such as wars and natural disasters.
    c. pay the President's salary.
    d. operate the government and pay previous years' debt.

_____ 36. During the cold war, American relations with the Soviet Union were dominated by
      a. détente.   c. containment.
      b. foreign aid.   d. collective security.

_____ 37. A major feature of American foreign policy since World War II has been
      a. deterrence.
      b. the Roosevelt Corollary to the Monroe Doctrine.
      c. support for the League of Nations.
      d. renewed isolationism.

_____ 38. Which historic world event finally ended the United States' commitment to a policy of isolationism?
      a. World War II   c. the Korean War
      b. the Vietnam War   d. the Persian Gulf War

_____ 39. When President Nixon visited China to discuss foreign policy and represent the United States at ceremonial gatherings with Chinese leaders, what two presidential roles was he fulfilling?
      a. chief of state and commander in chief
      b. chief legislator and chief diplomat
      c. chief administrator and chief legislator
      d. chief of state and chief diplomat

_____ 40. What power is each President exercising in these three statements?
      (1) Roosevelt sent the Great White Fleet around the world.
      (2) Washington participated in the Whiskey Rebellion of 1794.
      (3) Truman used nuclear weapons.

      a. chief diplomat   c. commander in chief
      b. leader of the free world   d. representative signatory of treaties

UNIT 5—THE JUDICIAL BRANCH

Multiple Choice
Identify the letter of the choice that best completes the statement or answers the question.

MAIN IDEAS

_____ 1. One weakness of the Articles of Confederation was that
a. it established a dual court system.
b. it did not provide for a national judiciary.
c. Congress could create only a few lower federal courts.
d. the jurisdiction of the Supreme Court was not clearly defined.

_____ 2. Which of the following federal courts exercises both original and appellate jurisdiction?
a. the Supreme Court
b. court of appeals
c. district court
d. the Court of Appeals for the Federal Circuit

_____ 3. Most importantly, the Supreme Court is called the High Court because it is the
a. best court in the country.
b. only court established by the Constitution.
c. first court in which most of the important federal cases are heard.
d. last court in which federal questions can be decided.

_____ 4. The Court of Appeals for the Federal Circuit differs from the other 12 federal courts of appeals because it
a. does not hear appeals from regulatory agencies.
b. can have original jurisdiction over federal cases.
c. hears cases from across the country.
d. only hears appeals from the Supreme Court.

_____ 5. The term of office for constitutional court judges is determined by
a. the Constitution.   c. the Department of Justice.
b. Congress.   d. the President.

_____ 6. The power of judicial review is held
a. exclusively by the Supreme Court.
b. only by federal courts.
c. by most federal and State courts.
d. only by courts with appellate jurisdiction.

_____ 7. Which of the following statements about civil rights is NOT true?
    a.   Each person's rights are relative to the rights of others.
    b.   Rights sometimes conflict with one another.
    c.   Some rights may be limited in wartime.
    d.   Rights are extended only to citizens.

_____ 8. Which of the following statements about prior restraint is TRUE?
    a.   Prior restraints are usually upheld by the Supreme Court.
    b.   The Constitution guarantees the right of prior restraint.
    c.   The Supreme Court has only rarely upheld prior restraints.
    d.   Prior restraints are necessary to prevent censorship.

_____ 9. Laws against seditious speech have been upheld by the Supreme Court if they
    a.   disagree with the government in public.
    b.   urge people to vote against the government.
    c.   urge people to overthrow the government.
    d.   support the party out of power.

_____ 10. Government has the right to make reasonable rules regulating assemblies
    a.   to uphold its limits on free speech.
    b.   to protect against the inciting of violence or the endangerment of life.
    c.   in situations that may involve protest against government policies.
    d.   if rules are applied individually regarding content.

_____ 11. The Due Process Clause guarantees that
    a.   the National Government will not interfere with constitutional rights.
    b.   States are not bound by their State constitutions in matters of individual rights.
    c.   States will not deny people any basic or essential liberties.
    d.   State governments will police the National Government.

_____ 12. Which of the following statements about commercial speech is TRUE?
    a.   It is legal to print false or misleading advertising only to benefit government-funded products.
    b.   Cigarette ads are permitted on radio and television.
    c.   Federal law forbids pharmacies from advertising prescription drug prices.
    d.   Commercial speech is protected by the 1st and 14th amendments.

_____ 13. Which has received the most limited 1st Amendment protection?
    a.   radio and television   c.   movies
    b.   magazines   d.   newspapers

____ 14. Individual rights were included in the Constitution because
    a.   conflicts between individuals and the government remained unsolved.
    b.   the people demanded a listing of rights.
    c.   the distinction between civil rights and civil liberties had to be made.
    d.   people did not want the government to have any authority over them.

____ 15. The 10 amendments known as the Bill of Rights were originally intended as restrictions against
    a.   the already existing States.
    b.   any new States that would enter the Union.
    c.   the new National Government.
    d.   both the National Government and State governments.

____ 16. Under the Establishment Clause, the government still has the power to do all of the following EXCEPT
    a.   use tax money to pay for busing students to parochial schools.
    b.   provide public funds for some uses in church-related schools.
    c.   establish an acceptable voluntary prayer for use in public schools.
    d.   exercise control over public, seasonal displays.

____ 17. In deciding cases involving laws against sedition, the Supreme Court has
    a.   developed the "clear and present danger" rule.
    b.   established the excessive entanglement standard.
    c.   upheld the Alien and Sedition acts of 1798.
    d.   upheld the constitutionality of all such laws.

____ 18. The Free Exercise Clause gives people the right to
    a.   assemble on private property.
    b.   hold any religious beliefs.
    c.   offend public morals.
    d.   violate criminal law in the name of religion.

____ 19. The main reason that there is no exact definition of the due process guarantees is that the
    a.   Constitution is too specific.
    b.   guarantees protect citizens against unfair processes, but not unfair laws.
    c.   The Supreme Court only defines the guarantees on a case-by-case basis.
    d.   courts do not want to give away too much specific information to potential lawbreakers.

____ 20. The right to privacy inherent in the concept of due process has been applied with the most controversy recently in cases involving
    a.   abortion.   c.   bearing arms.
    b.   searches and seizures.   d.   school attendance.

____ 21. A(n) ____, requires the police to bring a prisoner before the court and explain why he or she should not be released.
   a.   writ of habeas corpus
   b.   bill of attainder
   c.   ex post facto law
   d.   indictment

____ 22. To have a fair trial, a person is guaranteed all of the following EXCEPT
   a.   trial within a reasonable time.
   b.   trial by a jury.
   c.   adequate defense.
   d.   media coverage if demanded.

____ 23. The main reason the Constitution dealt specifically with the crime of treason was that
   a.   treason was not considered a serious crime before the Constitution was written.
   b.   treason is a crime against the country, not against individuals.
   c.   the Framers knew the charge of treason can be used for political reasons.
   d.   the Framers wanted to prevent all treason in order to protect the democracy.

____ 24. Which of the following was declared by the Supreme Court to be "cruel and unusual punishment"?
   a.   denying inmates needed medical treatment
   b.   use of the electric chair as a form of execution
   c.   placing two inmates in a cell built for one
   d.   use of the firing squad as a form of execution

____ 25. The guarantee against double jeopardy protects a person from being tried
   a.   for more than one crime committed at any one time.
   b.   twice for the same crime.
   c.   for a crime the person did not commit.
   d.   for a federal crime in a State court.

____ 26. The inclusion of two due process clauses in the Constitution reflects the fact that
   a.   due process has two quite different meanings.
   b.   the Constitution is written poorly in regards to due process.
   c.   due process is very easy to define.
   d.   the Bill of Rights is for the National Government, and the 14th Amendment is for the States and their local governments.

____ 27. The 13th Amendment forbids
   a.   any form of military service.
   b.   slavery and most forms of involuntary servitude.
   c.   the draft.
   d.   all of the above.

_____ 28. In *Furman* v. *Georgia*, 1972, the Court ruled that
   a.   the death penalty is "cruel and unusual punishment."
   b.   existing death penalty laws were unconstitutional because they gave too much discretion to judges and juries.
   c.   putting two prisoners in a cell built for one is considered cruel and unusual punishment.
   d.   States can impose the death penalty for the sale of narcotics.

_____ 29. Which of the following statements about the 4th Amendment is TRUE?
   a.   It applies only to the States.
   b.   It prohibits all arrests made without a warrant.
   c.   It has been of little importance in our history.
   d.   It forbids unreasonable searches and seizures.

_____ 30. The writ of habeas corpus is intended to prevent
   a.   a prisoner from being tried for the same crime twice.
   b.   the accused from being brought before a judge.
   c.   the accused from being unjustly arrested and imprisoned without cause.
   d.   defendants from being denied a lawyer.

_____ 31. The 6th Amendment's guarantee of a speedy and public trial is aimed at
   a.   deterring potential criminals by fear of swift and certain punishment.
   b.   trying those accused of crimes without undue delay and avoiding secret trials.
   c.   eliminating overcrowded dockets in the nation's criminal courts.
   d.   preventing jurors from being unduly influenced by public opinion.

_____ 32. The only crime that is specifically defined in the Constitution is
   a.   espionage.   c.   forceful government overthrow.
   b.   sabotage.   d.   treason.

_____ 33. Which is the MOST accurate description of the way minority groups historically have been treated in the United States?
   a.   with complete equality
   b.   with reluctance to accept their equality
   c.   with a sincere recognition of their cultural differences
   d.   with willing acceptance of immigrants, but only forced acceptance of those minorities already residing in the United States

_____ 34. In regard to the issue of equality, the Constitution states that
   a.   all people are equal in all ways.
   b.   slaves should be equal to free people.
   c.   no person can be denied equal protection of the laws.
   d.   government cannot draw distinctions between persons and groups.

_____ 35. A person can become a citizen of the United States by all of the following means EXCEPT
    a. being born in the United States.
    b. being born beyond American jurisdiction to American parents.
    c. by an act of Congress or a treaty.
    d. illegally crossing the Mexican border into Texas.

_____ 36. In the past, women have been denied which of the following?
    a. the right to own property   c. suffrage
    b. educational opportunities   d. all of the above

_____ 37. The continuing theme of immigration policy in the United States has been to
    a. allow all refugees a safe haven.
    b. help many from other countries become citizens of the United States.
    c. exert limited control over who can enter the country.
    d. adapt regulations to fit changing conditions at a particular time.

_____ 38. Citizenship by birth is determined by the rules
    a. of naturalization and denaturalization.
    b. of jus soli and jus sanguinis.
    c. set forth in the amendments to the Constitution.
    d. of individual or collective naturalization.

_____ 39. The first major Supreme Court case that challenged affirmative action was
    a. *University of California* v. *Bakke.*
    b. *Brown* v. *Board of Education of Topeka.*
    c. *Plessy* v. *Ferguson.*
    d. *Hoyt* v. *Florida.*

_____ 40. Which of the following statements does NOT accurately describe the Supreme Court decision in *Brown* v. *Board of Education of Topeka?*
    a. It reversed the earlier decision in *Plessy* v. *Ferguson.*
    b. It held that segregation by race in public education is unconstitutional.
    c. It quickly brought about integration of schools in this country.
    d. It struck down the separate-but-equal doctrine in education.

UNIT 6—COMPARATIVE POLITICAL AND ECONOMIC SYSTEMS

Multiple Choice
Identify the letter of the choice that best completes the statement or answers the question.

MAIN IDEAS

_____ 1. The structure of the Chinese Communist Party is similar to that of
   a.   Mexico's Institutional Revolutionary Party.
   b.   the former Soviet Union's Communist Party.
   c.   the Japan Democratic Party.
   d.   the United Kingdom's Conservative Party.

_____ 2. The customs and practices of British government are derived from
   a.   the ruling monarch.
   b.   nine law lords.
   c.   a written constitution.
   d.   an unwritten constitution.

_____ 3. Under the process of devolution, the British Parliament has reserved for itself exclusive powers in the areas of
   a.   agriculture, education, and housing.
   b.   defense, foreign policy, and macroeconomic policy.
   c.   health services, education, and culture.
   d.   education, the environment, and health services.

_____ 4. The main difference between the constitutions of China and the United States is that
   a.   the United States Constitution cannot be changed.
   b.   the Chinese constitution is intended to be fundamental law.
   c.   the Chinese constitution reflects current government policy, not fundamental law.
   d.   the current Chinese constitution is only about 5 years old.

_____ 5. In Mexico's local government system, each state has all of the following EXCEPT
   a.   a separate president.
   b.   a unicameral legislature.
   c.   a system of state courts.
   d.   a state constitution.

_____ 6. Which political party has dominated Japanese politics since the end of World War II?
   a.   Japan Communist Party
   b.   New Frontier Party
   c.   Liberal Democratic Party
   d.   Japan Socialist Party

_____ 7. The collapse of the Soviet communist government was mainly due to
   a.   the outpouring of support for the coup in 1991.
   b.   Gorbachev's refusal to restructure the political system.
   c.   the election of Boris Yeltsin as President.
   d.   its own inability to accommodate the rising demand for widespread democratic reform.

____ 8. Japan is a unitary state, so its individual prefectures have
   a. much less power than the individual States in the United States.
   b. much more power than the individual States in the United States.
   c. about the same amount of power as the States.
   d. no power at all.

____ 9. Like the Constitution of the United States, Mexico's fundamental law establishes a national government
   a. with three separate, independent branches.
   b. headed by the leader of the majority party in the General Congress.
   c. headed by a unicameral General Congress, holding both executive and legislative power.
   d. with one branch, headed by the president, holding all powers.

____ 10. Today, China regards the Republic of Taiwan as
   a. a sovereign ally.   c. its province.
   b. an independent nation.   d. an autonomous region.

____ 11. Which of the following best describes the written portion of the British constitution?
   a. It is known as the conventions of the constitution.
   b. It is derived from past usages and traditions.
   c. It consists of the customs and practices of British politics.
   d. It consists of historic charters, acts of Parliament, and innumerable court decisions.

____ 12. Which of the following statements best describes the regional and local government structure present in Mexico today?
   a. Mexico is a collection of autonomous provinces, each with their own president and legislative bodies, eliminating the need for a local government structure.
   b. Mexico is divided into 31 states and 1 Federal District, with each state providing for a governor, unicameral legislature, and state courts.
   c. Mexico is a communist society, and because of this local government is subject to the direct control of the ruling party.
   d. Mexico is split between two Federal Districts, with each sharing authoritarian control and giving little governing power to units of local government.

____ 13. In the United Kingdom, courts and judges may never overrule the policies of
   a. the executive branch.   c. the Constitution.
   b. regional courts.   d. Parliament.

____ 14. What is the role of the emperor in Japanese government today?
   a. He serves as an advisor to the prime minister.
   b. He is commander in chief of the military.
   c. He serves as the symbol of the people's unity.
   d. He may vote to break a tie in the House of Councillors.

_____ 15. In October of 1949, _____ became the first leader of the People's Republic of China.
    a.   Chiang Kai-shek
    b.   Mao Zedong
    c.   Emperor Jimmu
    d.   Josef Stalin

_____ 16. Which of the following was Gorbachev's program of perestroika designed to address?
    a.   the decline in worker motivation and output
    b.   the inflexibility of the market economy
    c.   the corruption of the Marxian ideals associated with economic and social equality
    d.   the decline of economic growth and productivity throughout the Soviet Union

_____ 17. An advantage of a sole proprietorship is that
    a.   it draws on the capital resources of more than one person.
    b.   the owner is not personally responsible for its debts.
    c.   it can continue indefinitely after the owner dies.
    d.   the owner can make business decisions quickly.

_____ 18. Private individuals and companies decide what products to manufacture and what prices to charge for goods and services in a
    a.   market economy.
    b.   socialist economy.
    c.   welfare state.
    d.   command economy.

_____ 19. Marx envisioned communism in its final form as a
    a.   triumph for the free enterprise system.
    b.   religion for the bourgeoisie.
    c.   dictatorship of the proletariat.
    d.   free and classless society.

_____ 20. Karl Marx wrote *The Communist Manifesto* as
    a.   a direct attack on democracy.
    b.   a call to improve market economies.
    c.   an anti-tax revolt.
    d.   a call to all oppressed workers to free themselves from "capitalistic enslavement."

_____ 21. Because private enterprise and government coexist together in American economic life, the economic system is called a
    a.   federalist economy.
    b.   mixed economy.
    c.   purely socialist economy.
    d.   a quasi-command economy.

_____ 22. A distinctive feature of capitalism is that
    a.   the goods and services produced by capital become public property.
    b.   private individuals are prohibited from owning productive property.
    c.   most productive property is owned and operated by private individuals or companies.
    d.   only public officials can decide how productive property is to be used.

____ 23. The amount of money earned after subtracting the costs associated with that earning is known
as
a.   trust.   c.   investment.
b.   monopoly.   d.   profit.

____ 24. Which of the following include the basic factors of production?
a.   land, labor, management, and capital
b.   capitalists, trust, monopoly, and labor
c.   agriculture, mining, and forestry
d.   goods and services

____ 25. The type of business organization whose income is subject to two taxes, one on profits and
one on dividends, is a
a.   sole proprietorship.   c.   corporation.
b.   partnership.   d.   monopoly.

____ 26. Which of the following actions or policies was based primarily on Marx's theory of socialism?
a.   Deng's introduction of limited free enterprise in China
b.   Stalin's practice of giving party officials all possible economic and social advantages
c.   Gorbachev's introduction of the policies of *perestroika*
d.   Communist party control of all social, political, and economic institutions

____ 27. In a mixed economy,
a.   private enterprise competes with the government for economic dominance.
b.   the government and private enterprise coexist as major participants.
c.   all business enterprises are publicly owned, but privately managed.
d.   the government directs all economic activity.

____ 28. Public ownership of productive property combined with large-scale centralized planning is a
representative trait of which economic system?
a.   communism   c.   democracy
b.   capitalism   d.   free enterprise system

____ 29. The type of business organization that is owned by two or more individuals sharing the
collective resources of those individuals is known as a
a.   corporation.   c.   sole proprietorship.
b.   partnership.   d.   monopoly.

____ 30. The ideas of socialism developed in large part as a
a.   reaction to poverty and hardships caused by the Industrial Revolution.
b.   result of the struggle for bourgeoisie independence from the proletariat elite.
c.   peaceful alternative to the violence associated with democracy.
d.   voluntary movement towards a publicly managed free enterprise economy.

____ 31. In contrast to republics such as the United States and France, Britain's system of government is based on a monarchy. How is a monarchy's leader different from a republic's leader?
   a. A monarchy has a leader appointed by the House of Lords, and a republic has an elected leader.
   b. A monarchy has a hereditary ruler, and a republic has an elected leader.
   c. A monarchy has a parliamentary leader, and a republic has an appointed leader.
   d. A monarch possesses divine rule, and a republic has no leader.

____ 32. How does Japan's National Diet compare to the central institution of British government?
   a. Both parliaments can force the Prime Minister to resign or to dissolve the House of Representatives and call for an early election.
   b. Britain's constitution is unwritten, while Japan's constitution was written under the watchful eye of American authorities.
   c. Both parliaments are bicameral, including an upper house and a lower house, and the lower house wields the greater power.
   d. Both parliaments include a House of Councillors and a House of Representatives.

____ 33. What forces caused the downfall of the Soviet Union?
   a. Gorbachev's *glasnost* led to a wave of democratization in Eastern Europe, Yeltsin challenged Gorbachev and the Soviet government, and three Baltic republics departed from the Union.
   b. *Glasnost* appointed a new secretary, Gorbachev, who quickly gained the respect of rebel nations Lithuania, Latvia, and Estonia, who announced their independence by mid-1990.
   c. Yeltsin's *perestroika* led to a new wave of communism that spread rapidly across Eastern Europe, and thousands of protesters took to the streets of Moscow in support of the Union's breakup.
   d. Communist Party leaders, disheartened by years of failed democratic reforms, fueled an independence movement that gained strength in the Baltic Soviet states.

____ 34. Which of the following BEST characterize China today?
   a. economic reforms and limits on human rights
   b. economic downfall and civil rights
   c. communism and human rights initiatives
   d. political dissent and democracy

____ 35. Which of the following best completes this sentence? Laissez-faire theory holds that government should play a very limited role in ____.
   a. foreign affairs   c. national defense
   b. society   d. law enforcement

____ 36. Which of the following does NOT belong in a description of Mexico's government and politics?
    a. three independent branches of government—executive, legislative and judicial
    b. a bicameral legislature composed of a Senate and a Chamber of Deputies
    c. divided into 31 states and one Federal District
    d. a multi-party system, with no party having complete control of the government

____ 37. Although the American economic system is private in character, economists usually describe the nation as having a mixed economy. What two elements coexist in this mixture?
    a. corporate sponsorship and sole proprietorship
    b. partnerships and corporations
    c. private enterprise and governmental participation
    d. public works and private enterprise

____ 38. What sweeping social changes led to the development of present-day socialism?
    a. The Renaissance movement and its emphasis on private ownership led many Western Europeans to embrace socialism's capitalist ideologies.
    b. The Industrial Revolution's movement from an agricultural to an industrial economy led many people in Western Europe to fear its "capitalist enslavement."
    c. The severe poverty caused by communist mismanagement led many to adopt a socialist form of government and its private enterprise ideals.
    d. The welfare system in Eastern Europe collapsed, fueled public unrest, added scores of citizens to welfare lines, and flooded the market economy with unemployed workers.

____ 39. Why would socialism be an especially attractive philosophy for a developing nation?
    a. The depressed economy of a developing nation naturally rebounds when placed under foreign control and ownership, reducing investments internationally while stimulating growth.
    b. By limiting the layers of bureaucracy, socialist countries minimize decision making and improve individual initiative, which can boost a developing nation's growth.
    c. Socialism appeals to leaders who want to mobilize an entire nation behind a single program of industrial growth, channeling investment into the parts of the economy that are most essential.
    d. With a tradition of locally controlled, large-scale industry, developing nations are attracted to the small-scale, government-owned industry representative of socialism.

____ 40. Mao Zedong's patriotic movement appealed to
    a. the intellectual elite.   c. the Chinese peasantry.
    b. prosperous businessmen.   d. the United States.

UNIT 7—STATE AND LOCAL GOVERNMENT

Multiple Choice
Identify the letter of the choice that best completes the statement or answers the question.

MAIN IDEAS

_____ 1. Which of the following is NOT true of each State's constitution?
   a. Each State constitution details the means by which it may be amended.
   b. Each State constitution takes priority over all provisions of federal law.
   c. Each State constitution contains a bill of rights guaranteeing certain rights to the public.
   d. Each State constitution distributes power among the three branches of State government.

_____ 2. All of the following are nonlegislative powers held by State legislatures EXCEPT the
   a. power to approve certain gubernatorial appointments.
   b. power of impeachment.
   c. power to make and revise constitutional amendments.
   d. police power.

_____ 3. Today, the most widely used method for selecting judges to sit in State and local courts is
   a. popular election.   c. selection by the governor.
   b. selection by the legislature. d. selection by judicial commission.

_____ 4. A serious criminal case may be heard without a petit jury if the
   a. judge orders that a grand jury be used instead.
   b. State permits the prosecuting attorney to use information instead.
   c. accused waives the right to a trial by jury.
   d. jurors waive their right to hear and decide the case.

_____ 5. Which State was the first in which popular approval played a direct role in the adoption and ratification of a State constitution?
   a. Massachusetts   c. Georgia
   b. New York   d. Connecticut

_____ 6. According to the Texas constitution, if a governor resigns or leaves office midterm, the _____ serves the remainder of his or her term.
   a. attorney general   c. lieutenant governor
   b. secretary of state   d. president of the senate

_____ 7. The _____ is the usual device by which new State constitutions are written and older constitutions revised.
   a. constitutional convention   c. selection by legislature
   b. selection by public initiative d. selection by governor

____ 8. How long are the terms of State legislators?
   a. 1 or 2 years
   b. 2 or 3 years
   c. 1 or 3 years
   d. 2 or 4 years

____ 9. Which action is based on the police power of State legislatures?
   a. impeaching a State judge
   b. imposing a meals tax
   c. requiring the use of seat belts
   d. proposing a new State constitution

____ 10. The fundamental laws of each State are
   a. established by the governor.
   b. determined by State courts.
   c. never subject to change.
   d. the State constitution.

____ 11. Most State legislatures today are
   a. unicameral.
   b. bicameral.
   c. nonpartisan.
   d. relatively powerless.

____ 12. Which of the following is responsible for the formal interpretation of a State's constitutional and statutory law?
   a. the governor
   b. the lieutenant governor
   c. the secretary of state
   d. the attorney general

____ 13. ____ is a procedure by which the legislature may remove a governor from office before the completion of his or her regular term.
   a. Referendum
   b. Initiative
   c. Recall
   d. Impeachment and conviction

____ 14. The names of potential jurors are often selected from
   a. telephone books.
   b. postal service lists.
   c. political party rolls.
   d. voter's and driver's license lists.

____ 15. All of the following include examples of the common functions of counties EXCEPT the
   a. maintaining of jails and correctional facilities.
   b. assessing of property for tax purposes.
   c. registering and recording deeds and birth certificates.
   d. dividing of land into residential, commercial, and industrial zones.

____ 16. The largest expenditure in the Texas state budget is for ____.
   a. law enforcement
   b. public works
   c. education
   d. medical assistance

_____ 17. City zoning is most often opposed on the grounds that it
  a. typically raises property values.
  b. is used primarily to benefit real estate developers.
  c. denies people the right to use their property as they choose.
  d. has been declared unconstitutional by the Supreme Court.

_____ 18. Many weaknesses of county government are caused by the lack of
  a. a centralized executive authority.
  b. power to pass laws.
  c. elected officers authorized to perform countywide duties.
  d. commissions authorized to regulate county services.

_____ 19. Which of the following includes examples of the ways in which metropolitan areas attempt to meet fiscal challenges?
  a. the annexation of outlying areas
  b. the creation of special districts in heavily populated urban areas
  c. the increase of authority given to local county governments
  d. all of the above

_____ 20. Which statement is true about all counties in the United States?
  a. Their size is based on the size of the State.
  b. Their size is based on the population of the State.
  c. They can only be created by the State.
  d. They serve only a judicial function.

_____ 21. The main purpose of a city's charter is to
  a. establish the city as a legal body.
  b. set out the city's basic laws.
  c. provide a forum for public debate.
  d. provide for the election of city officers.

_____ 22. The main reason that States hold many important powers is that the
  a. Framers distrusted a strong central government.
  b. Constitution does not grant many States' rights.
  c. Constitution describes a unitary State.
  d. States have accrued these powers over the years.

_____ 23. The purpose of a State budget is to
  a. give the appearance of order to a chaotic series of steps in spending.
  b. list expenses that have already been made.
  c. divide the previous year's surplus among the local units of government.
  d. decide which agencies receive money and how much.

____ 24. State constitutions may limit taxes on
   a.   interstate commerce.
   b.   federal property.
   c.   religious and other nonprofit groups.
   d.   purely private purposes.

____ 25. At the State and local level, the first step in the typical budget process is that
   a.   the budget is considered part-by-part by the legislature.
   b.   spending estimates are reviewed by an executive budget agency.
   c.   the governor reviews spending estimates and presents the information to the legislature.
   d.   each agency prepares estimates of its needs and expenditures for the upcoming year.

____ 26. As a type of local government, special districts are created to
   a.   serve rural areas only.
   b.   coordinate county services only.
   c.   meet specified public needs.
   d.   meet general public needs.

____ 27. The planning method most cities rely on to classify and control land use within their boundaries is called
   a.   zoning.
   b.   due process.
   c.   urbanization.
   d.   environmental protection.

____ 28. In most States, people buying new cars must pay both
   a.   sales and property taxes.
   b.   income and sales taxes.
   c.   estate and license taxes.
   d.   amusement and property taxes.

____ 29. The dramatic shift from a rural to an urban population was first made possible on a large scale by the
   a.   stagecoach.
   b.   steam engine.
   c.   automobile.
   d.   airplane.

____ 30. The United States Constitution reserves to the States all powers not delegated to Congress or denied to the States, meaning that the States
   a.   hold almost no power.
   b.   have little responsibility to the Federal Government.
   c.   hold a great number of powers.
   d.   have complete authority over the Federal Government.

INTERPRETING DIAGRAMS
Use the diagram to answer the following questions.

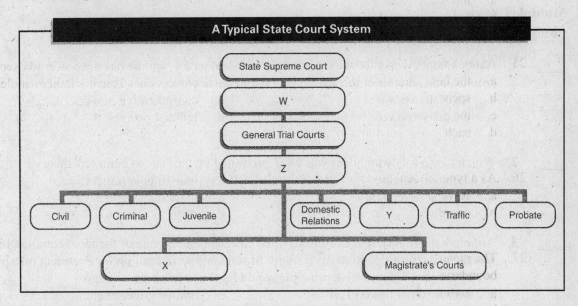

____ 31. Which label should appear at the place marked by the letter *W*?
  a. Court of Appeals
  b. Small Claims
  c. Municipal Courts
  d. Justice Courts

____ 32. What structure does the diagram represent?
  a. the appeals process under criminal law
  b. the organization of a typical city court system
  c. the organization of a typical State court system
  d. the structure of judicial appointment under the Missouri plan

____ 33. Which label should appear at the place marked by the letter *X*?
  a. Justice Courts
  b. Small Claims
  c. Municipal Courts
  d. Court of Appeals

____ 34. If the decision of an appellate court is appealed, the case then goes before
  a. a magistrates court.
  b. a municipal court.
  c. a general trial court.
  d. the State supreme court.

FIRST-SEMESTER EXAM

Multiple Choice
Identify the letter of the choice that best completes the statement or answers the question.

_____ 1. Isaiah's father works for the government of a democracy, and he has the power to execute, enforce, and administer the law. What type of basic powers does Isaiah's father handle?
 a. legislative powers   c. confederative powers
 b. executive powers   d. judicial powers

_____ 2. Which of the following ideas was NOT promoted by the "social contract" theory?
 a. common defense   c. limited government
 b. popular sovereignty   d. individual rights

_____ 3. Although the first state constitutions differed considerably, one of the most common features was the principle of popular sovereignty. If someone were running for President on a platform of popular sovereignty, what principle would he or she be emphasizing?
 a. separation of powers   c. limited government
 b. consent of citizens   d. civil rights

_____ 4. Although the Articles of Confederation established a relationship among the states, the 1780s was a critical period because it exposed weaknesses in the document. What resulted from these weaknesses?
 a. mass migration from southern states to western territories
 b. economic and political instability in every state
 c. unfair taxation of some citizens without representation in Congress
 d. a banking system inadequate to fulfill every state's needs

_____ 5. What did the smaller states fear during the framing of the Constitution that led to a series of compromise proposals?
 a. They were worried that the larger states would have the power to regulate interstate commerce.
 b. They were worried that the larger states would have greater representation in Congress and would dominate the government.
 c. They were worried that the smaller states would be unable to participate in the slave trade.
 d. They were worried that the larger states would have fewer separations of power and would use this loophole to gain control of the Senate.

_____ 6. The concept known as _____ means that basic powers are distributed among three distinct branches of government.
 a. constitutionalism   c. limited government
 b. separation of powers   d. distributed government

_____ 7. In 1999, President Clinton used his executive powers to send troops to the Yugoslav province of Kosovo. Considering that only Congress can declare war, how was President Clinton able to send troops into combat without such a declaration?
   a. As the President of the United States, Clinton had exclusive authority over Congress.
   b. As commander in chief, the President can declare war if conditions set forth in the War-Peace Agreement are met.
   c. President Clinton was able to use his powers of veto to overturn Congress's decision not to send troops.
   d. As the commander in chief, Clinton used his power to make an informal amendment without congressional approval.

_____ 8. The Constitution delegates powers to the National Government, powers to the States, and powers that both have. Which of the following belongs in the shaded area of the Venn diagram that illustrates the division of powers?

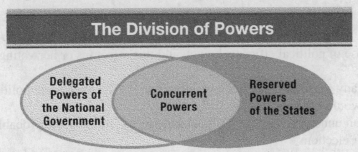

The Division of Powers

Delegated Powers of the National Government | Concurrent Powers | Reserved Powers of the States

   a. borrow money   c. coin money
   b. regulate foreign trade   d. establish public schools

_____ 9. What clause of the Constitution states that no State can draw unreasonable distinctions between its own residents and those persons who live in other States?
   a. privileges and immunities clause   c. interstate compact clause
   b. full faith and credit clause   d. extradition and immunities clause

_____ 10. What does the Constitutional principle of judicial review mean?
   a. People are the source of any and all government power.
   b. Government is restricted in what it may do, and each individual has rights the government cannot take away.
   c. the power of a court to determine the constitutionality of a governmental action
   d. system of overlapping the powers of the three branches of government to check the actions of the others

_____ 11. Which set of words best completes this sentence? Although the United States is a democracy, Americans live in a ____, in which multiple groups interact and share political power.
   a. confrontational nation   c. dualistic society
   b. multiparty consensus   d. pluralistic society

_____ 12. Which of the following is a reason for voter registration?
  a. to prove a potential voter's ability to read and write
  b. to prove payment of property taxes
  c. to discourage women from voting
  d. to prevent fraudulent voting

_____ 13. The Civil Rights Act of 1964 continued a pattern established by earlier Civil Rights legislation that emphasized
  a. legislative action to overcome racial barriers and the use of state courts to protect minority voter literacy testing.
  b. judicial action to overcome racial barriers and the use of federal court-ordered injunctions.
  c. voting rights for all Americans, including women and African Americans.
  d. protections for the rights of minority voters that established the minimum voting age of 18.

_____ 14. If someone has no sense of political efficacy, how would this affect his or her voting behavior?
  a. The person lacks any sense of his or her own influence or effectiveness in politics, so the person probably would not vote.
  b. The person feels an unnatural sense of political superiority, so he or she probably would vote only in major elections.
  c. The person does not understand politics, so he or she probably would vote only in school board elections.
  d. The person feels that the political process is not as fair as it once was, so he or she probably would vote for campaign reform.

_____ 15. Why is a straw vote highly unreliable?
  a. It falsely assumes that a small sample of responses will provide a fairly accurate picture of public opinion.
  b. It falsely assumes that a relatively large number of responses will provide a fairly accurate picture of public opinion.
  c. It falsely assumes that the people polled are all of the same general income and education level.
  d. It falsely assumes that everyone in a single geographic area shares the same political opinions.

_____ 16. What impact does the mass media have on the public agenda?
  a. It has no impact because top political figures do not pay attention to these sources.
  b. It has made candidates far more dependent on party organizations.
  c. It tells people how and for whom to vote.
  d. It focuses the public's attention on specific issues.

_____ 17. About 300,000 physicians belong to the American Medical Association (AMA). Which of the following best describes this group?
   a. The AMA is an economic special interest group that pressures the government to increase aid to students and the underprivileged.
   b. The AMA is a business special interest group that elects members to political office in the hopes of influencing public policy.
   c. The AMA is a labor economic interest group that raises funds to rewrite worldwide legislation and foreign policy.
   d. The AMA is an economic professional interest group that impacts public policy for the welfare of the profession and its members.

_____ 18. Today, lobbyists are people who
   a. are hired by the government to act as watchdogs over the political process.
   b. work within the governmental process to affect policies.
   c. work outside the political system to meet a group's needs.
   d. have no loyalties to any particular issue.

_____ 19. Which is NOT a reason why the Framers of the Constitution set up a bicameral legislature?
   a. They were familiar with the British form of government, which had two houses.
   b. They created two houses to settle the conflict between the larger and smaller states.
   c. They expected a legislature with two houses would streamline the process of government.
   d. They favored a Congress with two houses in order that one house might act as a check on the other.

_____ 20. In 1997, 26-year-old Representative Harold Ford Jr. became a member of the 105th Congress. What happened the year before this that made his election possible?
   a. Congress passed the Voter Registration Act of 1997.
   b. Congress lowered the age of a member of the House to 26.
   c. He had lived in the state of Tennessee for at least seven years.
   d. He celebrated his twenty-fifth birthday.

_____ 21. Why is a senator's term in office different in length than that of a representative's?
   a. Senators' terms are shorter because they require less experience than representatives do.
   b. Senators' terms are longer so they can be staggered; therefore, a majority of senators is always experienced.
   c. Senators' terms are limited to only one term in office; therefore their term in office is longer.
   d. Senators' terms are shorter in order to make sure they accurately represent their constituents.

_____ 22. How does the Constitution differ in the powers it gives Congress to tax and to borrow?
    a. Congress's power to tax is unlimited, and there are no limits on borrowing.
    b. The Constitution limits Congress's power to tax, but there are no limits on borrowing.
    c. Congress's power to borrow is not unlimited, but its power to tax is.
    d. The Constitution limits Congress's power to tax and it bars Congress from borrowing.

_____ 23. Congress shares powers with the President in the field of foreign affairs. What other powers do Congress and the President share?
    a. judicial powers   c. territorial powers
    b. postal powers   d. war powers

_____ 24. What is the implied power expressed by the Necessary and Proper Clause in the Constitution?
    a. Congress's ability to make laws is severely limited by the Constitution.
    b. Congress is given limited authority to interpret reserved powers.
    c. Congress must follow a concrete interpretation of the Constitution.
    d. Congress can make any law that it deems appropriate.

_____ 25. What nonlegislative action has the Senate performed only during the presidencies of Andrew Johnson and Bill Clinton?
    a. voted to acquit   c. withdrew deficit financing
    b. voted to impeach   d. declared bankruptcy

_____ 26. The Constitution makes no mention of them, yet these bodies play an essential role in the lawmaking process. Their job is to sift through and decide the fate of bills. What are they?
    a. quorums   c. standing committees
    b. committees of the whole   d. conference committees

_____ 27. Which of the following is NOT a federal crime specifically mentioned in the Constitution?
    a. counterfeiting   c. piracy
    b. treason   d. kidnapping

_____ 28. As directed by Article I of the Constitution, when are congressional seats reapportioned?
    a. following each Presidential election   c. after each decennial census
    b. by popular demand   d. every six years

_____ 29. The purpose of a filibuster is to
    a. invoke the rule of cloture.   c. allow quorum calls.
    b. overrule a Presidential veto.   d. prevent action on a bill.

____ 30. What event brought *McCulloch* v. *Maryland* before the Supreme Court?
   a.   The state of Maryland based its congressional districts on race.
   b.   The state of Maryland attempted to tax federal bank notes.
   c.   The state of Maryland governor disagreed with the power of Congress to regulate interstate commerce.
   d.   The state of Maryland refused to follow the federal standards of weights and measures.

____ 31. Among the broad purposes of the United States government spelled out in the Preamble to the Constitution is the obligation to
   a.   keep the executive and legislative branches of government separate.
   b.   create an autocratic form of government.
   c.   defend the country against Americans who oppose its policies.
   d.   provide for justice and the people's general welfare.

____ 32. The theory underlying modern democracies was developed to challenge the idea that
   a.   those of royal birth have absolute authority to rule.
   b.   the people as a whole are the sole source of political power.
   c.   the head of a family, clan, or tribe has the natural right to govern.
   d.   the strongest person or group has the right to control others by force.

____ 33. A federal government is one in which
   a.   all power is concentrated in the central government.
   b.   limited powers are assigned to a central agency by independent states.
   c.   power is divided between a central government and local governments.
   d.   powers are divided between a legislative branch and an executive branch.

____ 34. Which of the following statements is NOT true of parliamentary government?
   a.   The executive is chosen by the legislature.
   b.   The legislature is subject to the direct control of the executive.
   c.   The prime minister and cabinet are part of the legislative branch.
   d.   The prime minister and cabinet must resign if they lose the support of a majority of the legislature.

____ 35. The individual 50 States lack which basic characteristic of a state?
   a.   government   c.   Constitution
   b.   sovereignty   d.   defined population

____ 36. The Internet seems especially suited to satisfy which of these needs in a democracy?
   a.   to control the lives of citizens
   b.   to be informed about the many different institutions and policies of the government
   c.   the need for accurate, and always reliable, information on which to base decisions
   d.   the need for an uneducated elite to run the government

____ 37. In a democracy, the will of the majority
      a. cannot be changed or improved upon.
      b. is not open to compromise.
      c. rarely leads to satisfactory policy decisions.
      d. cannot be used to deprive rights to a member of a minority group.

____ 38. Which idea is NOT included in the Declaration of Independence?
      a. People have certain natural rights.
      b. God gives certain people the right to govern.
      c. Government can exist only with the people's permission.
      d. The people may change or abolish the government.

____ 39. All of the following influenced the Framers in developing the Constitution EXCEPT
      a. State constitutions.
      b. John Locke's *Two Treatises of Government.*
      c. Virginia's royal charter.
      d. British tradition.

____ 40. Which colony was founded mainly as a place for personal and religious freedom?
      a. Virginia   c. Massachusetts
      b. Georgia   d. New York

____ 41. A major objective of both the Annapolis Convention and the Philadelphia Convention was to
      a. determine how the States should be represented in Congress.
      b. recommend a federal plan for regulating interstate trade.
      c. raise an army for quelling incidents like Shay's Rebellion.
      d. limit the growing power of the National Government.

____ 42. The government set up by the Articles of Confederation had
      a. no legislative or judicial branch.
      b. only a legislative and an executive branch.
      c. only a legislative branch, consisting of a unicameral Congress.
      d. only a legislative branch, consisting of a bicameral Congress.

____ 43. Which was an achievement of the Second Continental Congress?
      a. preparing a Declaration of Rights
      b. raising an American army
      c. establishing a strong central government
      d. passing the Intolerable Acts

____ 44. Parliament first limited the power of the Crown under the
      a. Intolerable Acts.   c. Stamp Act of 1765.
      b. Petition of Right.   d. English Bill of Rights.

_____ 45. *The Federalist* was written to
  a. win support for the Constitution in New York.
  b. expose the lack of civil liberties protected in the Constitution.
  c. urge ratification of the Constitution in Virginia.
  d. condemn the Constitution for the absence of any mention of God.

_____ 46. By the mid-1700s, British rule in the colonies was marked by
  a. allowing a certain degree of self-rule to the colonists.
  b. imposing harsh and restrictive trade practices.
  c. passing increasingly high taxes.
  d. forcing the colonies to attack other colonial powers.

_____ 47. Much of the Declaration of Independence consists of
  a. statements of the desire to separate from England.
  b. lists of the rights of all people.
  c. complaints of the wrongs done to the colonists.
  d. threats of revenge for English mistreatment.

_____ 48. The success of which plan led to the Constitutional Convention of 1787?
  a. Albany Plan of Union
  b. Second Continental Congress's "plan of confederation"
  c. interstate plan for regulating trade between Virginia and Maryland
  d. compromise reached between the Virginia and New Jersey plans

_____ 49. Supreme Court rulings have been key to broadening the scope of which expressed power?
  a. the postal power   c. the commerce power
  b. the power to tax   d. eminent domain

_____ 50. The powers of Congress are affected by all of the following EXCEPT what the
  a. Constitution expressly says Congress may do.
  b. Constitution says only the States may do.
  c. States' constitutions say Congress may do.
  d. Constitution is silent about.

_____ 51. The Supreme Court ruling in *Gibbons* v. *Ogden* expanded the
  a. currency power by including paper money as legal tender.
  b. power to tax by allowing a tax on incomes.
  c. commerce power to include all commercial interactions.
  d. power over territories to include the taking of private property.

_____ 52. According to the Constitution, who has the sole power to impeach the President?
  a. The House of Representatives   c. the Supreme Court
  b. the Vice President   d. State courts

_____ 53. Which of the following is an example of the investigatory powers of Congress?
    a.   accepting a treaty made by the President
    b.   the power to regulate commerce with foreign nations
    c.   the power to lay and collect taxes
    d.   gathering information useful in making legislative decisions

_____ 54. All the following expressed powers belong to Congress EXCEPT
    a.   the power to declare war.   c.   the power to naturalize citizens.
    b.   the power to tax exports.   d.   the power to raise an army.

_____ 55. Under the Constitution, Congress has the sole power to
    a.   act as the commander in chief.   c.   declare war.
    b.   meet with foreign leaders.   d.   none of the above.

_____ 56. All the following are implied powers of Congress EXCEPT the power to
    a.   set maximum work hours.   c.   fund education programs.
    b.   restrict arms sales.   d.   censor radio and TV programs.

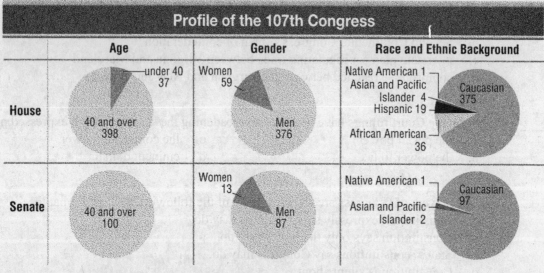

SOURCE: Congressional Research Service

_____ 57. Study the circle graph of race and ethnic backgrounds for the 107th Congress. How does racial and ethnic diversity differ between the House and the Senate?
    a.   The House has Hispanic and African American representatives, but the Senate has none.
    b.   The House has a greater percentage of Caucasians.
    c.   The Senate has Asians and Pacific Islanders, but the House has African Americans.
    d.   The House has more Native Americans than does the Senate.

_____ 58. Although members of Congress are elected to represent the people, they are not a representative cross-section of the American people. How do the circle graphs of the 107th Congress illustrate this fact?
    a. They show that there are no African American members of Congress.
    b. They show that everyone in the House is over 40.
    c. They show that there are fewer women in the Senate than there are in the House.
    d. They show that most members are white, over 40, and male.

_____ 59. Why are political parties considered a vital link between the people and their government?
    a. The only way to be nominated for President is by affiliation with a major political party.
    b. They are considered the principal means by which the will of the people is made known to the government.
    c. They are considered the only way of decentralizing the power of the government.
    d. Because the United States is a democracy, political parties are considered the only way to bring people together.

_____ 60. Why should the major political parties be concerned about a strong minor party candidate on the ballot for President?
    a. Historically, fewer people vote when there are more than two candidates on the ballot.
    b. Minor party candidates are unable to take clear-cut stands on controversial issues.
    c. Campaign funds are divided between all candidates, so there is less money available to the major parties.
    d. Minor party candidates can pull a large number of votes from either party, causing an upset.

_____ 61. If you wanted to run for President of the United States, but you did not win a party's endorsement, what could you do to keep yourself in the running?
    a. get the endorsement of a state legislature
    b. commandeer a national party convention
    c. match government mandated campaign funds
    d. announce yourself as a candidate for President

MAIN IDEAS

_____ 62. The Full Faith and Credit Clause of the Constitution provides that
    a. Congress may not pass laws that conflict with State laws.
    b. State laws must be uniform.
    c. State laws and court decisions must generally be honored by other States.
    d. agreements made between the States must first be approved by Congress.

INTERPRETING DIAGRAMS
Use the diagram to answer the following questions.

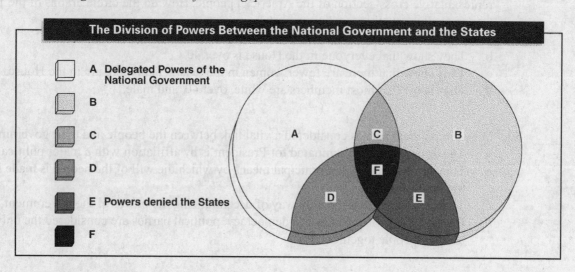

The Division of Powers Between the National Government and the States

A Delegated Powers of the National Government

B

C

D

E Powers denied the States

F

_____ 63. What label should appear at the place marked by the letter *D*?
    a.   Concurrent Powers
    b.   Powers reserved to the States
    c.   Powers denied both the National Government and the States
    d.   Powers denied the National Government

_____ 64. What label should appear at the place marked by the letter *B*?
    a.   Concurrent Powers
    b.   Powers denied the National Government
    c.   Powers reserved to the States
    d.   Powers denied both the National Government and the States

_____ 65. What label should appear at the place marked by the letter *C*?
    a.   Concurrent Powers
    b.   Powers denied the National Government
    c.   Powers reserved to the States
    d.   Powers denied both the National Government and the States

_____ 66. What label should appear at the place marked by the letter *F*?
    a.   Concurrent Powers
    b.   Powers reserved to the States
    c.   Powers denied both the National Government and the States
    d.   Powers denied the National Government

_____ 67. The label *Powers reserved to the States* belongs at the place marked by
    a.   the letter *F*.   c.   the letter *C*.
    b.   the letter *B*.   d.   the letter *D*.

_____ 68. The label *Powers denied to the National Government* should be placed at

a.   the letter *E*.

b.   the letters *D* and *B*.

c.   the letters *C* and *F*.

d.   the letter *D*.

SECOND-SEMESTER EXAM

Multiple Choice
Identify the letter of the choice that best completes the statement or answers the question.

_____ 1. When President Nixon visited China to discuss foreign policy and represent the United States at ceremonial gatherings with Chinese leaders, what two presidential roles was he fulfilling?
   a.   chief of state and commander in chief
   b.   chief legislator and chief diplomat
   c.   chief administrator and chief legislator
   d.   chief of state and chief diplomat

_____ 2. The election of 1800 exposed serious flaws in the election system, which had worked fine for the 1789 and 1792 elections. Which of the following is one of three new elements that were introduced into the presidential selection process after the election of 1800?
   a.   the elimination of party nominations for the presidency and vice presidency
   b.   the automatic casting of electoral votes in line with electors' pledges
   c.   the electors' free agent system
   d.   the 11th Amendment electoral college rule

_____ 3. What do voters do in a state presidential primary?
   a.   elect a President and a Vice President
   b.   express a preference for a presidential candidate
   c.   establish each party's platform
   d.   meet in a caucus to decide which candidates to vote for

_____ 4. Why could presidential candidate "A" lose a presidential election despite receiving more votes than candidate "B"?
   a.   Candidate "A" received more electoral votes than candidate "B," but the votes were from smaller states.
   b.   Candidate "B" received more electoral votes than Candidate "A."
   c.   Candidate "A" won the majority of electoral votes but lost the popular vote.
   d.   Candidate "B" won the popular vote, even though Candidate "A" received more electoral votes.

_____ 5. The Constitution requires the President to execute all federal laws, but what can the President do if he or she has a fundamental disagreement with a particular federal law?
   a.   declare the law unconstitutional and send it back to the courts
   b.   ignore the law
   c.   decide how and in what way to apply the law
   d.   veto the law

© Pearson Education, Inc.

_____ 6. What power is each President exercising in these three statements?
 (1) Roosevelt sent the Great White Fleet around the world.
 (2) Washington participated in the Whiskey Rebellion of 1794.
 (3) Truman used nuclear weapons.

    a. chief diplomat   c. commander in chief
    b. leader of the free world   d. representative signatory of treaties

_____ 7. President's legislative power : veto ; _____ : clemency
    a. President's judicial power   c. President's imperial power
    b. President's executive power   d. President's wartime power

_____ 8. How is the President's Cabinet chosen?
    a. appointed by the President and confirmed by Congress
    b. appointed by the President and confirmed by the Senate
    c. appointed by the President and confirmed by the Supreme Court
    d. appointed by Congress and confirmed by the President

_____ 9. Independent regulatory commissions differ from other independent agencies because
    a. they are protected from the influence of partisan politics.
    b. they administer programs similar to those of the Cabinet departments.
    c. they are largely beyond the reach of presidential direction and control.
    d. all members are from a single political party, usually the President's.

_____ 10. What important reforms were made in the civil service system in the 1880s after President Garfield was fatally shot?
    a. The Washington, D.C., civil service initiative was expanded nationwide.
    b. The postal service was privatized.
    c. Civil service workers who broke the law were subject to being deported.
    d. Reforms made merit the basis for hiring, promotion, and other personnel actions.

_____ 11. What word BEST completes this sentence? World War II led to a historic shift in American foreign policy from a position of _____ to one of internationalism.
    a. nationalism   c. conservatism
    b. regionalism   d. isolationism

_____ 12. How are federal district courts different from courts of appeals?
  a. Appeals courts were created by the Constitution and are the final authority on questions of federal law, and district courts have original jurisdiction over most cases heard in the federal courts.
  b. Appeals courts deal with civil and criminal cases from the local and state level, and district courts are gatekeepers that relieve the Supreme Court of the burden of hearing cases from other courts.
  c. Appeals courts are gatekeepers that relieve the Supreme Court of the burden of hearing cases from other courts, and district courts have original jurisdiction over most cases heard in the federal courts.
  d. Appeals courts limit their caseloads to appeals involving constitutional questions and interpretations of federal law, and district courts deal with civil and criminal cases from the local and state levels.

_____ 13. How did *Marbury* v. *Madison* illustrate the Supreme Court's power of judicial review?
  a. The Court determined that Madison intended to deceive the lower courts in his appeal to the Supreme Court.
  b. The Court ruled that Madison must perform any acts he has a clear legal duty to perform.
  c. The Court agreed with Marbury's argument that Madison's actions were of criminal intent.
  d. The Court refused Marbury's request because he based his case on a law the Court concluded was unconstitutional.

_____ 14. What does the Due Process Clause of the Fourteenth Amendment say?
  a. Each State shall . . . restrict any person from testifying against himself or herself because of due process.
  b. No State shall . . . deprive any person of life, liberty, or property, without due process of law.
  c. Due process . . . is an unalienable right given to citizens as a result of the Civil Rights Act of 1964.
  d. Due process . . . allows each State to accept public acts, records, and judicial proceedings as a matter of due process.

_____ 15. What reasoning did the Supreme Court give for its decision on whether burning an American flag is a form of speech protected by the Constitution?
  a. The Court reasoned that flag burning is like commercial speech and, prior to the 1970s, was not protected by the First and Fourteenth Amendments.
  b. The Court reasoned that burning an American flag was an act of sedition and treason, which were serious crimes noted in the Alien and Sedition Acts of 1798.
  c. The Court reasoned that the government may not prohibit the expression of an idea simply because society finds the idea offensive, a concept protected by the First Amendment.
  d. The Court reasoned that burning an American flag was not protected by the shield laws that recognize free, symbolic speech as an inalienable right.

____ 16. Which of the following groups of protesters is NOT protected by the First Amendment?
   a. those handing out leaflets in front of an abortion clinic
   b. those participating in a Ku Klux Klan rally
   c. those carrying signs demanding the resignation of the police chief
   d. those asking people on the street to sign a petition

____ 17. Why did the Supreme Court add the idea of substantive due process to the original notion of procedural due process at the end of the nineteenth century?
   a. They reasoned that the Fifth Amendment denies people the right to property without due process.
   b. They reasoned that fair procedures are of little value if they are used to administer unfair laws.
   c. They reasoned that due process laws are unconstitutional unless the crime is substantial.
   d. They reasoned that procedural due process laws are not broad enough to be significant.

____ 18. A police officer wants to search a suspect's home. How does he or she justify a search warrant?
   a. The police officer must possess the exclusionary rule.
   b. The police officer must possess a writ of assistance.
   c. The police officer must have probable cause.
   d. The police officer must have an arrest warrant.

____ 19. Which of these statements involves the writ of *habeas corpus*?
   a. A court cannot punish someone for a crime for which no law exists.
   b. A person cannot be punished for an act without a court trial.
   c. An officer must show cause for why a prisoner should not be released.
   d. A person cannot be tried twice for the same crime.

____ 20. Which of the following constitutes cruel and unusual punishment according to the Supreme Court?
   a. mandatory life sentence for a noncapital crime
   b. two prisoners inhabiting a cell meant for one person
   c. preventative detention
   d. narcotics addiction defined as a crime, rather than an illness

_____ 21. How did the Civil Rights Act of 1964 and the Civil Rights Act of 1968 influence the Federal Government's policy of affirmative action?
   a. These Acts upheld the Court's belief that discrimination was wrong, and affirmative action was the government's way of making states pay for the abuses of the past.
   b. These Acts challenged long-standing discrimination, and affirmative action was the government's way of taking steps to remedy the effects of past discriminations.
   c. These Acts challenged long-standing discrimination, and affirmative action allowed the government to create reverse discrimination, which pleased all ethnic groups.
   d. These Acts affirmed discrimination as unconstitutional; however, affirmative action created a loophole that would not allow schools to deny admittance of students because of quotas.

_____ 22. The Supreme Court decision that ended legalized segregation in the public schools was
   a. *Hoyt* v. *Florida.*
   b. *Orr* v. *Orr.*
   c. *Brown* v. *Board of Education of Topeka.*
   d. *Alexander* v. *Holmes County Board of Education.*

_____ 23. In contrast to republics such as the United States and France, Britain's system of government is based on a monarchy. How is a monarchy's leader different from a republic's leader?
   a. A monarchy has a leader appointed by the House of Lords, and a republic has an elected leader.
   b. A monarchy has a hereditary ruler, and a republic has an elected leader.
   c. A monarchy has a parliamentary leader, and a republic has an appointed leader.
   d. A monarch possesses divine rule, and a republic has no leader.

_____ 24. Which of the following does NOT belong in a description of Mexico's government and politics?
   a. three independent branches of government—executive, legislative and judicial
   b. a bicameral legislature composed of a Senate and a Chamber of Deputies
   c. divided into 31 states and one Federal District
   d. a multi-party system, with no party having complete control of the government

_____ 25. What forces caused the downfall of the Soviet Union?
   a. Gorbachev's *glasnost* led to a wave of democratization in Eastern Europe, Yeltsin challenged Gorbachev and the Soviet government, and three Baltic republics departed from the Union.
   b. *Glasnost* appointed a new secretary, Gorbachev, who quickly gained the respect of rebel nations Lithuania, Latvia, and Estonia, who announced their independence by mid-1990.
   c. Yeltsin's *perestroika* led to a new wave of communism that spread rapidly across Eastern Europe, and thousands of protesters took to the streets of Moscow in support of the Union's breakup.
   d. Communist Party leaders, disheartened by years of failed democratic reforms, fueled an independence movement that gained strength in the Baltic Soviet states.

_____ 26. Which of the following BEST characterize China today?
    a. economic reforms and limits on human rights
    b. economic downfall and civil rights
    c. communism and human rights initiatives
    d. political dissent and democracy

_____ 27. Which of the following best completes this sentence? Laissez-faire theory holds that government should play a very limited role in _____.
    a. foreign affairs   c. national defense
    b. society   d. law enforcement

_____ 28. Although the American economic system is private in character, economists usually describe the nation as having a mixed economy. What two elements coexist in this mixture?
    a. corporate sponsorship and sole proprietorship
    b. partnerships and corporations
    c. private enterprise and governmental participation
    d. public works and private enterprise

_____ 29. What sweeping social changes led to the development of present-day socialism?
    a. The Renaissance movement and its emphasis on private ownership led many Western Europeans to embrace socialism's capitalist ideologies.
    b. The Industrial Revolution's movement from an agricultural to an industrial economy led many people in Western Europe to fear its "capitalist enslavement."
    c. The severe poverty caused by communist mismanagement led many to adopt a socialist form of government and its private enterprise ideals.
    d. The welfare system in Eastern Europe collapsed, fueled public unrest, added scores of citizens to welfare lines, and flooded the market economy with unemployed workers.

_____ 30. Karl Marx predicted that workers in different countries would revolt and embrace communism. Which of the following did he NOT anticipate?
    a. Communism would be hastened by revolution.
    b. Economic growth and productivity would decline.
    c. Social classes would vanish and all property would be communal.
    d. People's national loyalties and sentiments would intensify.

_____ 31. Mao Zedong's patriotic movement appealed to
    a. the intellectual elite.   c. the Chinese peasantry.
    b. prosperous businessmen.   d. the United States.

_____ 32. Which of the following are the two kinds of formal changes that have been used to amend state constitutions?
    a. proposals and ratifications   c. initiatives and ballots
    b. conventions and legislatures   d. amendments and revisions

____ 33. What is the difference between statutory law and administrative law?
   a. Administrative law is based on the provisions of the United States Constitution and the 50 state constitutions; statutory law is unwritten, judgment law that developed over time.
   b. Statutory law consists of the laws enacted by legislative bodies; administrative law is composed of the rules, orders, and regulations that are issued by federal, state, or local executive offices.
   c. Administrative law consists of the laws enacted by legislative bodies; statutory law is based on the provisions of the United States Constitution and the 50 state constitutions.
   d. Statutory law is composed of the rules, orders, and regulations that are issued by federal, state, or local executive offices; administrative law is unwritten, judgement law that developed over time.

____ 34. If someone is indicted on criminal charges, the trial may be heard by a petit jury. What does this jury do?
   a. This jury decides on the punishment the accused person will receive, but its decision is directed by state law.
   b. This jury decides whether evidence against a person is sufficient to justify a trial; their decision must be unanimous.
   c. This jury decides whether criminal intent is involved, and five of the six jurors must agree on a verdict.
   d. This jury reviews the evidence, decides the disputed facts, and must reach a unanimous verdict.

____ 35. Which form of city government has an elected mayor as the chief executive and an elected council as the legislative body?
   a. strong-mayor government
   b. weak-council government
   c. mayor-council government
   d. mayor-commission government

____ 36. What is the main purpose of city zoning?
   a. It is a phase of city planning that helps ensure the orderly growth of a city.
   b. It encourages random, widespread growth of cities.
   c. It allows cities to raise taxes and fund education.
   d. It creates tax-free regions based on the economic growth and stability of an area.

____ 37. How is the Texas state budget process different from that of most states?
   a. The legislature, not the governor, prepares the state's budget.
   b. The governor and legislature share responsibility for preparing the budget.
   c. The legislature can veto the governor's budget but cannot administer funds.
   d. The governor does not take part in preparing budgets or administering funds.

_____ 38. Which of the following is NOT true of each State's constitution?
   a. Each State constitution details the means by which it may be amended.
   b. Each State constitution takes priority over all provisions of federal law.
   c. Each State constitution contains a bill of rights guaranteeing certain rights to the public.
   d. Each State constitution distributes power among the three branches of State government.

_____ 39. The fundamental laws of each State are
   a. established by the governor.
   b. determined by State courts.
   c. never subject to change.
   d. the State constitution.

_____ 40. Most State legislatures today are
   a. unicameral.
   b. bicameral.
   c. nonpartisan.
   d. relatively powerless.

INTERPRETING TABLES
Use the table to answer the following questions.

PUBLIC DEBT OF THE UNITED STATES				
Fiscal Year	Debt (billions)	Per Capita (dollars)	Interest Paid (billions)	Percent of Federal Outlay
1870	$2.4	$61.06	—	—
1880	2.0	41.60	—	—
1890	1.1	17.80	—	—
1900	1.2	16.60	—	—
1910	1.1	12.41	—	—
1920	24.2	228	—	—
1930	16.1	131	—	—
1940	43.0	325	$1.0	10.5
1945	258.7	1,849	3.8	4.1
1950	256.1	1,688	5.7	13.4
1955	272.8	1,651	6.4	9.4
1960	284.1	1,572	9.2	10.0
1965	313.8	1,613	11.3	9.6
1970	370.1	1,814	19.3	9.9
1975	533.2	2,475	32.7	9.8
1980	907.7	3,985	74.9	12.7
1981	997.9	4,338	95.6	14.1
1982	1,142.0	4,913	117.4	15.7
1983	1,377.2	5,870	128.8	15.9
1984	1,572.3	6,640	153.8	18.1
1985	1,823.1	7,598	178.9	18.9
1986	2,125.3	8,774	190.2	19.2
1987	2,350.3	9,615	195.4	19.5
1988	2,602.3	10,534	214.1	20.1
1989	2,857.4	11,545	240.9	21.0
1990	3,233.3	13,000	264.8	21.1
1991	3,665.3	14,436	285.4	21.5

Source: Department of the Treasury

____ 41. The total public debt first went over $900 billion in

a.   1945.   c.   1979.
b.   1960.   d.   1980.

____ 42. The interest paid
a.   reached over $5,526 billion by 1998.
b.   never increased by more than $10 billion per year.
c.   increased by over $363 billion since 1940.
d.   exceeded $100 billion in 1981.

____ 43. In what year did the public debt take the greatest percent of total federal outlay?
a.   1970   c.   1991
b.   1986   d.   1955

____ 44. The total public debt in 1990 was ____ billion.
a. $3,233.3   c. $907.7
b. $2,857.4   d. $3,665.3

____ 45. The interest paid on public debt has
a.   remained about the same since 1980.
b.   increased steadily from 1940.
c.   fluctuated greatly between 1940 and 1991.
d.   decreased steadily from 1940.

____ 46. The difference between per capita public debt in 1900 and in 1991 was
a. $98.85.   c. $14,419.40.
b. $2,856.20.   d. $11,561.60.

INTERPRETING CHARTS
Use the chart to answer the following questions.

Constitutional Protections for Persons Accused of Crime

W | Informed right to counsel and to remain silent | X | Grand jury or prosecutor weighs evidence | Informed of charge by indictment or information | Speedy and public trial by impartial jury | Y | No excessive fine or cruel and unusual punishment | Z

Writ of habeas corpus if illegally detained

No unreasonable search and seizure

No excessive bail

No self-incrimination
Assistance of counsel
Confront witnesses

No double jeopardy

____ 47. In the chart, what label should appear in the box marked *W*?
a.   Right to appeal
b.   Verdict of jury
c.   No third degree or coerced confession
d.   Arrest on warrant or probable cause

_____ 48. Another label for the second box from the top would be
    a. Exclusionary rule in effect.
    b. Police follow Miranda Rule.
    c. Defendant invokes the 5th Amendment.
    d. Informed of custody rights.

_____ 49. The second box from the bottom describes rights protected by
    a. preventive detention.
    b. the 8th Amendment.
    c. the Miranda Rule.
    d. the use of two-stage trials.

_____ 50. Which label should appear in the box marked *Z*?
    a. Right to appeal
    b. Verdict of jury
    c. No third degree or coerced confessions
    d. Arrest on warrant or probable cause

_____ 51. The fifth box lists two ways the accused can be informed of charges. What is a third way?
    a. presentment
    b. writ of habeas corpus
    c. Supreme Court ruling
    d. bill of attainder

_____ 52. Which label should appear in the box marked *Y*?
    a. Right to appeal
    b. Verdict of jury
    c. No third degree or coerced confession
    d. Arrest on warrant or probable cause

INTERPRETING MAPS
Use the map to answer the following questions.

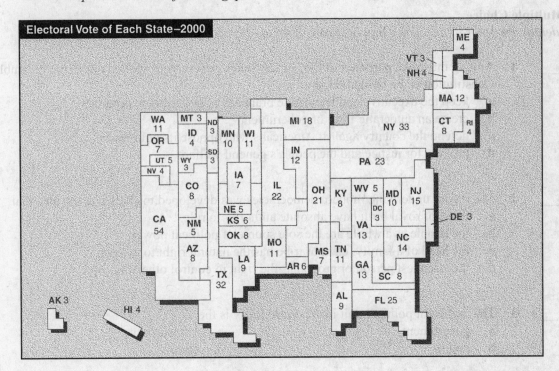

Electoral Vote of Each State—2000

_____ 53. The number of electoral votes that Iowa has is
a. five.
b. seven.
c. nine.
d. twelve.

_____ 54. The States with the largest electoral vote include
a. Pennsylvania and Illinois.
b. Alaska and Hawaii.
c. Texas and Florida.
d. California and New York.

_____ 55. The figure 11 for Washington indicates that the State has 11
a. senators.
b. representatives.
c. presidential electors.
d. districts.

_____ 56. On this map, the size of each State is determined by
a. the number of its electoral votes.
b. its population.
c. its number of members in the Senate.
d. its actual physical area.

WHOLE-COURSE EXAM

Multiple Choice
Identify the letter of the choice that best completes the statement or answers the question.

_____ 1. Among the broad purposes of the United States government spelled out in the Preamble to the Constitution is the obligation to
  a. keep the executive and legislative branches of government separate.
  b. create an autocratic form of government.
  c. defend the country against Americans who oppose its policies.
  d. provide for justice and the people's general welfare.

_____ 2. The theory underlying modern democracies was developed to challenge the idea that
  a. those of royal birth have absolute authority to rule.
  b. the people as a whole are the sole source of political power.
  c. the head of a family, clan, or tribe has the natural right to govern.
  d. the strongest person or group has the right to control others by force.

_____ 3. The dominant political unit in the world today is the
  a. government.   c. Constitution.
  b. nation.   d. state.

_____ 4. A federal government is one in which
  a. all power is concentrated in the central government.
  b. limited powers are assigned to a central agency by independent states.
  c. power is divided between a central government and local governments.
  d. powers are divided between a legislative branch and an executive branch.

_____ 5. Which of the following is among the characteristics of a state?
  a. population   c. government
  b. territory   d. all of the above

_____ 6. All political powers in a state are concentrated at the central level under which form of government?
  a. federal   c. unitary
  b. confederate   d. executive

_____ 7. Which of the following illustrates the concept of equality of opportunity?
  a. Public schools may not exclude students because of their sex or race.
  b. Citizens must obey the tax laws but may work to change them.
  c. Government may limit the beliefs and ideas of individuals.
  d. Senators consider testimony both for and against Supreme Court nominees.

____ 8. In the charter colonies, most governmental matters were handled by
    a.   the British monarch.   c.   a proprietor.
    b.   Parliament.   d.   the colonists.

____ 9. Which idea is NOT included in the Declaration of Independence?
    a.   People have certain natural rights.
    b.   God gives certain people the right to govern.
    c.   Government can exist only with the people's permission.
    d.   The people may change or abolish the government.

____ 10. All of the following influenced the Framers in developing the Constitution EXCEPT
    a.   State constitutions.
    b.   John Locke's *Two Treatises of Government*.
    c.   Virginia's royal charter.
    d.   British tradition.

____ 11. Which colony was founded mainly as a place for personal and religious freedom?
    a.   Virginia   c.   Massachusetts
    b.   Georgia   d.   New York

____ 12. Which feature did the State constitutions and the Articles of Confederation have in common?
    a.   royal governors
    b.   bill of rights
    c.   principle of popular sovereignty
    d.   a strong executive elected by popular vote

____ 13. Which of these State constitutions is the oldest and still in force today?
    a.   Massachusetts   c.   New Hampshire
    b.   South Carolina   d.   Virginia

____ 14. A major objective of both the Annapolis Convention and the Philadelphia Convention was to
    a.   determine how the States should be represented in Congress.
    b.   recommend a federal plan for regulating interstate trade.
    c.   raise an army for quelling incidents like Shay's Rebellion.
    d.   limit the growing power of the National Government.

____ 15. The government set up by the Articles of Confederation had
    a.   no legislative or judicial branch.
    b.   only a legislative and an executive branch.
    c.   only a legislative branch, consisting of a unicameral Congress.
    d.   only a legislative branch, consisting of a bicameral Congress.

____ 16. *The Federalist* was written to
   a. win support for the Constitution in New York.
   b. expose the lack of civil liberties protected in the Constitution.
   c. urge ratification of the Constitution in Virginia.
   d. condemn the Constitution for the absence of any mention of God.

____ 17. The success of which plan led to the Constitutional Convention of 1787?
   a. Albany Plan of Union
   b. Second Continental Congress's "plan of confederation"
   c. interstate plan for regulating trade between Virginia and Maryland
   d. compromise reached between the Virginia and New Jersey plans

____ 18. With the words, "We the People," the Constitution establishes its authority on the basis of
   a. popular sovereignty.   c. the separation of powers.
   b. the rule of law.   d. limited government.

____ 19. The informal amendment process
   a. involves changing the written words of the Constitution.
   b. has been used very little in the past 200 years.
   c. can occur only with the approval of the States.
   d. results from the daily experiences of government.

____ 20. Which of the following best describes the concept of limited government?
   a. Powers are divided among three independent branches of government.
   b. All political power belongs to the people.
   c. Government must operate within certain bounds set by the people.
   d. The people must behave according to rules set by the government.

____ 21. Which of the following is a method of formal amendment?
   a. proposal by three-fourths of the House of Representatives and ratification by conventions in three-fourths of State legislatures
   b. proposal by two-thirds of the Senate and ratification by two-thirds of State legislatures
   c. proposal by two-thirds of Congress and ratification by three-fourths of State legislatures
   d. all of the above

____ 22. Which of the following informal amendments was a result of party practices?
   a. the use of the electoral college as a "rubber stamp" for the popular vote
   b. the revised structure of the federal court system
   c. executive agreement
   d. the practice of senatorial courtesy

_____ 23. The basic constitutional rights of the people were FIRST set out in the
   a.   13th, 14th, and 15th amendments.
   b.   10th Amendment.
   c.   Bill of Rights.
   d.   Equal Rights Amendment.

_____ 24. The legislative branch can check the judicial branch by its power to
   a.   name federal judges.
   b.   remove judges through impeachment.
   c.   declare executive actions unconstitutional.
   d.   override a presidential veto.

_____ 25. The President's power to veto an act of Congress is an example of
   a.   executive agreement.   c.   checks and balances.
   b.   judicial review.   d.   limited government.

_____ 26. The Bill of Rights guarantees all of the following EXCEPT
   a.   fair treatment before the law.   c.   freedom of expression.
   b.   the right of women to vote.   d.   freedom of belief.

_____ 27. The system of federalism provides for all of the following EXCEPT
   a.   local action in matters of local concern.
   b.   a dual system of government.
   c.   uniform laws among the States.
   d.   strength through unity.

_____ 28. Concurrent powers are those that are
   a.   exercised simultaneously by the National and the State governments.
   b.   exercised by State governments alone.
   c.   exercised by the National Government alone.
   d.   denied to both the National and the State governments.

_____ 29. Local governments derive their power from
   a.   the Constitution and federal laws.
   b.   State constitutions and State laws.
   c.   both State constitutions and the National Government.
   d.   city and county governments.

_____ 30. Which of the following is an expressed power of the National Government?
   a.   the power to coin money   c.   the power to acquire territory
   b.   the power to license doctors   d.   the power to grant divorces

____ 31. The power of the National Government to coin money is
    a. an implied power.
    b. an inherent power.
    c. an expressed power.
    d. a concurrent power.

____ 32. Which of the following is NOT among the obligations that the National Government has to the States?
    a. protection against foreign attack and domestic violence
    b. guarantee of a representative form of government
    c. recognition of each State's legal existence and physical boundaries
    d. recognition of State constitutions as the supreme law of the land

____ 33. Which of the following is the basic characteristic of federalism?
    a. It divides power between a National Government and State governments.
    b. It gives most power to the National Government.
    c. It gives most power to local units of government.
    d. It encourages citizen participation in government.

____ 34. Which statement about local government is accurate?
    a. Local government has no relationship with State governments.
    b. Local government is an extension of the federal government.
    c. Local government is a subunit of State government.
    d. Local government supercedes the authority of State government.

____ 35. In the case of *McCulloch* v. *Maryland*, what was the Supreme Court ruling based upon?
    a. reserved powers
    b. Full Faith and Credit Clause
    c. Supremacy Clause
    d. interstate compacts

____ 36. In the United States, a political party is made up of a group of people who
    a. disagree on how to resolve the basic issues affecting the country.
    b. work to get candidates elected to political offices.
    c. work separately to support one major program or policy.
    d. support split-ticket voting.

____ 37. The national chairperson of a major political party
    a. organizes congressional campaigns.
    b. develops the platform upon which a presidential candidate runs.
    c. manages the party's headquarters.
    d. elects all members of the national committee.

_____ 38. People belong to a particular political party
    a. according to regulations of State law.
    b. voluntarily, because they made a personal choice.
    c. based on the location of the State in which they live.
    d. according to regulations of federal law.

_____ 39. Which of the following statements about Federalists is TRUE?
    a. They called for a strict interpretation of the Constitution.
    b. George Washington founded their party.
    c. They were generally supported by farmers.
    d. A strong national government was of great concern to them.

_____ 40. The two-party system developed in the United States mainly because
    a. the Constitution established a democratic government.
    b. conflicts about the Constitution created opposing viewpoints.
    c. leaders and voters agreed on the existence of two parties.
    d. it was voted on and approved by both houses of Congress.

_____ 41. In the past, some States limited voting rights by
    a. passing political socialization laws.   c. eliminating the literacy test.
    b. charging a poll tax.   d. overruling grandfather clauses.

_____ 42. The provisions of the Voting Rights Act of 1965 and its amendments of 1970, 1975, and 1982 apply to
    a. all national, State, and local elections.
    b. federal elections only.
    c. State and local elections only.
    d. all federal and State elections, but not to all local elections.

_____ 43. The expansion of suffrage in the United States
    a. was outlined in the text of the Constitution.
    b. was accomplished outside the United States legal system.
    c. is the subject of all constitutional amendments made since 1810.
    d. has been moved forward by amendments and civil rights acts.

_____ 44. Literacy tests worked to deny the right to vote to African Americans primarily because
    a. all white voters had higher literacy rates.
    b. the tests were only required in Southern States.
    c. African Americans were asked questions that were more difficult than those asked of prospective white voters.
    d. it was specifically provided for in the Constitution.

_____ 45. Which act first established a federal commission to investigate claims of individual voter discrimination?
    a. Civil Rights Act of 1957   c. Civil Rights Act of 1964
    b. Civil Rights Act of 1960   d. Voting Rights Act of 1965

_____ 46. All of the following have been used to keep African Americans from voting EXCEPT
    a. poll taxes.   c. federal court orders.
    b. literacy tests.   d. threats and social pressures.

_____ 47. The single most significant predictor of a person's partisan voting behavior is his or her
    a. party identification.   c. political efficacy.
    b. educational background.   d. perceptions of government.

_____ 48. The 15th Amendment, ratified in 1870, did not secure the right of African Americans to vote primarily because
    a. it did not state that voting rights could not be denied to African Americans.
    b. the Federal Government did not intervene to uphold the amendment.
    c. it was repealed by Congress shortly after ratification.
    d. it prevented State leaders from acting on behalf of potential voters who were being discriminated against.

_____ 49. Gerrymandering is unfair because
    a. no one has the right to divide electoral districts for elections.
    b. it sets district boundaries to decrease one group's voting strength.
    c. it makes voter registration difficult for uneducated white males.
    d. it increases the voting power of minority groups.

_____ 50. The nominating stage is important in the electoral process mostly because
    a. only Republicans and Democrats can take part in nominations.
    b. nominations set real limits to the choices voters can make in general elections.
    c. major party candidates exert more effort to win nominations than elections.
    d. in a democracy the general election is little more than a formality.

_____ 51. Voters are asked to complete election ballots in all of the following ways EXCEPT
    a. moving levers on a voting machine.   c. returning a mail-in ballot.
    b. marking a punch card.   d. raising hands at a public meeting.

_____ 52. Campaign contributions to a presidential candidate can
    a. come from any foreign country.   c. all be made anonymously.
    b. be for any amount of money.   d. be made by any American.

____ 53. The oldest form of the nominating process in the United States is
     a.   the convention.
     b.   a congressional caucus.
     c.   the direct primary.
     d.   self-announcement.

____ 54. The most costly items in a typical campaign budget today are
     a.   newspaper and magazine advertisements.
     b.   pamphlets and posters.
     c.   travel and entertainment.
     d.   television advertisements.

____ 55. Which of the following statements about PACs is FALSE?
     a.   They can raise funds only for presidential and congressional campaigns.
     b.   They distribute money to those candidates who are sympathetic to their policy goals.
     c.   They can give no more than $5,000 to any one federal candidate in an election.
     d.   They can give no more than $15,000 a year to a political party.

____ 56. In a closed primary
     a.   only declared party members may vote.
     b.   all qualified voters may vote.
     c.   voters must vote a split ticket.
     d.   voters must complete separate ballots for both parties.

____ 57. Which of the following is the earliest and one of the most significant agents in the political socialization process?
     a.   family
     b.   place of residence
     c.   group affiliation
     d.   gender

____ 58. The term "public opinion" is misleading because
     a.   opinions have no place in politics or government.
     b.   Americans belong to many different publics, each with a distinctive viewpoint.
     c.   most Americans consider political opinions to be a private matter.
     d.   no two people in the public really agree on any issue.

____ 59. The most reliable measure of public opinion is
     a.   straw votes.
     b.   quota samples.
     c.   scientific polls.
     d.   pressure groups.

____ 60. Which statement about the Senate is true?
     a.   It has two members from each State.
     b.   Its members are chosen by State legislatures.
     c.   Each member represents one congressional district.
     d.   Seats are apportioned among the States according to their populations.

_____ 61. The House may refuse to seat a member-elect only if he or she
    a. has engaged in disorderly behavior.
    b. has violated the code of ethics passed by the House in 1977.
    c. does not meet constitutional standards of age, citizenship, and residency.
    d. does not meet informal standards set by two-thirds of the members.

_____ 62. Which of the following is true of the House of Representatives?
    a. It currently has 100 members.
    b. The total number of seats in the House is fixed by the Constitution.
    c. The number of terms a representative may serve is fixed by the Constitution.
    d. Every State is represented by at least one member.

_____ 63. Which of the following is an informal qualification for the House of Representatives?
    a. must be at least 25 years old
    b. must have been a citizen of the United States for at least seven years
    c. must be an inhabitant of the State from which he or she is elected
    d. must currently reside in the district he or she represents

_____ 64. Senators are elected to serve
    a. two-year terms.   c. four-year terms.
    b. three-year terms.   d. six-year terms.

_____ 65. Which of the following is a qualification for senators?
    a. must have been born in the State from which elected
    b. must have a degree in law
    c. must have been a citizen for at least nine years
    d. must be at least 40 years old

_____ 66. All of the following are nonlegislative powers held by State legislatures EXCEPT the
    a. power to approve certain gubernatorial appointments.
    b. power of impeachment.
    c. power to make and revise constitutional amendments.
    d. police power.

_____ 67. Unlike a grand jury, a petit jury
    a. always has 12 jurors.
    b. is used only in civil cases.
    c. may question witnesses and summon others to testify against a suspect.
    d. is a trial jury used in both civil and criminal cases.

_____ 68. Today, the most widely used method for selecting judges to sit in State and local courts is
    a. popular election.   c. selection by the governor.
    b. selection by the legislature.   d. selection by judicial commission.

_____ 69. Which State was the first in which popular approval played a direct role in the adoption and ratification of a State constitution?
a. Massachusetts
b. New York
c. Georgia
d. Connecticut

_____ 70. According to the Texas constitution, if a governor resigns or leaves office midterm, the _____ serves the remainder of his or her term.
a. attorney general
b. secretary of state
c. lieutenant governor
d. president of the senate

_____ 71. The _____ is the usual device by which new State constitutions are written and older constitutions revised.
a. constitutional convention
b. selection by public initiative
c. selection by legislature
d. selection by governor

_____ 72. How long are the terms of State legislators?
a. 1 or 2 years
b. 2 or 3 years
c. 1 or 3 years
d. 2 or 4 years

_____ 73. The fundamental laws of each State are
a. established by the governor.
b. determined by State courts.
c. never subject to change.
d. the State constitution.

_____ 74. Most State legislatures today are
a. unicameral.
b. bicameral.
c. nonpartisan.
d. relatively powerless.

_____ 75. At the State and local level, the first step in the typical budget process is that
a. the budget is considered part-by-part by the legislature.
b. spending estimates are reviewed by an executive budget agency.
c. the governor reviews spending estimates and presents the information to the legislature.
d. each agency prepares estimates of its needs and expenditures for the upcoming year.

_____ 76. An unreasonable tax classification would be one aimed exclusively at
a. smokers.
b. beer drinkers.
c. people over 65.
d. insurance policy holders.

_____ 77. All of the following factors contributed to the growth of the nation's suburbs after World War II EXCEPT
   a. the desire for cheaper land.
   b. the need for less privacy.
   c. the need for newer and better public schools.
   d. the desire for a higher social status.

INTERPRETING TABLES

Use the chart to answer the following questions.

Forms of Government

Country	Where is the power?		What is the relationship between the legislative and executive branches?		Who can participate?	
	Unitary	Federal	Parliamentary	Presidential	Democracy	Dictatorship
Botswana	✓		✓		✓	
Brazil		✓		✓	✓	
Costa Rica	✓		✓		✓	
Cuba	✓		✓			✓
France	✓			✓	✓	
India		✓	✓		✓	
Syria	✓			✓		✓
United States		✓		✓	✓	

_____ 78. Which characteristic do the United States and Botswana have in common?
   a. Both countries are democratic.
   b. Both countries have a presidential form of government.
   c. Both countries have a unitary form of government.
   d. Both countries have parliamentary governments.

_____ 79. All of the following countries are democracies EXCEPT
   a. France.
   b. India.
   c. Syria.
   d. Brazil.

_____ 80. In which two countries do dictatorships exist?
   a. Cuba, France
   b. Brazil, India
   c. Cuba, Syria
   d. Botswana, Costa Rica

____ 81. What impact does the mass media have on the public agenda?
- a. It has no impact because top political figures do not pay attention to these sources.
- b. It has made candidates far more dependent on party organizations.
- c. It tells people how and for whom to vote.
- d. It focuses the public's attention on specific issues.

____ 82. Today, lobbyists are people who
- a. are hired by the government to act as watchdogs over the political process.
- b. work within the governmental process to affect policies.
- c. work outside the political system to meet a group's needs.
- d. have no loyalties to any particular issue.

____ 83. When President Nixon visited China to discuss foreign policy and represent the United States at ceremonial gatherings with Chinese leaders, what two presidential roles was he fulfilling?
- a. chief of state and commander in chief
- b. chief legislator and chief diplomat
- c. chief administrator and chief legislator
- d. chief of state and chief diplomat

____ 84. What do voters do in a state presidential primary?
- a. elect a President and a Vice President
- b. express a preference for a presidential candidate
- c. establish each party's platform
- d. meet in a caucus to decide which candidates to vote for

____ 85. What power is each President exercising in these three statements?
- (1) Roosevelt sent the Great White Fleet around the world.
- (2) Washington participated in the Whiskey Rebellion of 1794.
- (3) Truman used nuclear weapons.

- a. chief diplomat
- b. leader of the free world
- c. commander in chief
- d. representative signatory of treaties

____ 86. There are about 400 White House staff members working in the Executive Office of the president. Which of the following directly advises the President in all domestic, foreign, and military matters?
- a. Central Intelligence Agency
- b. National Security Council
- c. Foreign Affairs Council
- d. East Wing

____ 87. The Constitution specifies that spending measures must originate in the House of
          Representatives. According to tradition, how has this process begun?
    a. The White House Chief of Staff initiates the process by appointing the head of the Office
        of Management and Budget.
    b. The President initiates the process by submitting a budget at the beginning of each
        congressional session.
    c. Members of the Internal Revenue Service's budget committee initiate the process by
        submitting an outline of the budget to the President.
    d. The Office of Management and Budget initiates the process by submitting its Annual
        Report to the Nation.

____ 88. The Constitution creates two kinds of inferior Federal Courts. How do they differ?
    a. The Constitutional Courts exercise the broad judicial power of the United States, and the
        Special Courts have narrowly defined powers.
    b. The National Courts deal with national and international issues, and the State Courts
        hear most of the cases in the country dealing with public matters.
    c. The Supreme Federal Courts exercise the broad judicial power of the United States, and
        the Special Courts have narrowly defined powers.
    d. The High Courts exercise broad judicial power for the United States, and the Appeals
        Court handles cases that the lower courts are unable to settle.

____ 89. How did *Marbury* v. *Madison* illustrate the Supreme Court's power of judicial review?
    a. The Court determined that Madison intended to deceive the lower courts in his appeal to
        the Supreme Court.
    b. The Court ruled that Madison must perform any acts he has a clear legal duty to perform.
    c. The Court agreed with Marbury's argument that Madison's actions were of criminal
        intent.
    d. The Court refused Marbury's request because he based his case on a law the Court
        concluded was unconstitutional.

____ 90. What does the Due Process Clause of the Fourteenth Amendment say?
    a. Each State shall . . . restrict any person from testifying against himself or herself because
        of due process.
    b. No State shall . . . deprive any person of life, liberty, or property, without due process of
        law.
    c. Due process . . . is an unalienable right given to citizens as a result of the Civil Rights
        Act of 1964.
    d. Due process . . . allows each State to accept public acts, records, and judicial proceedings
        as a matter of due process.

91. Can religious groups meet at federally funded public high schools, despite the separation between church and state created by the Establishment Clause?
    a. Yes, they can meet there because the Supreme Court struck down a State law forbidding the teaching of scientific theory of evolution, finding the Establishment Law unconstitutional.
    b. Yes, they can meet there because the Equal Access Act of 1984 declares that federally funded public schools must allow student religious groups to meet in school on the same terms that it sets for other organizations.
    c. No, they cannot meet there because the Establishment Clause prohibits the "establishment of religion" on any publicly funded grounds.
    d. No, they cannot meet there because, although freedom of religion is guaranteed by the Constitution, the Free Exercise Clause denies Americans the right to practice that religion on government property.

92. Which of these statements involves the writ of *habeas corpus*?
    a. A court cannot punish someone for a crime for which no law exists.
    b. A person cannot be punished for an act without a court trial.
    c. An officer must show cause for why a prisoner should not be released.
    d. A person cannot be tried twice for the same crime.

93. What forces caused the downfall of the Soviet Union?
    a. Gorbachev's *glasnost* led to a wave of democratization in Eastern Europe, Yeltsin challenged Gorbachev and the Soviet government, and three Baltic republics departed from the Union.
    b. *Glasnost* appointed a new secretary, Gorbachev, who quickly gained the respect of rebel nations Lithuania, Latvia, and Estonia, who announced their independence by mid-1990.
    c. Yeltsin's *perestroika* led to a new wave of communism that spread rapidly across Eastern Europe, and thousands of protesters took to the streets of Moscow in support of the Union's breakup.
    d. Communist Party leaders, disheartened by years of failed democratic reforms, fueled an independence movement that gained strength in the Baltic Soviet states.

94. Which of the following BEST characterize China today?
    a. economic reforms and limits on human rights
    b. economic downfall and civil rights
    c. communism and human rights initiatives
    d. political dissent and democracy

95. Which of the following best completes this sentence? Laissez-faire theory holds that government should play a very limited role in ____.
    a. foreign affairs
    b. society
    c. national defense
    d. law enforcement

_____ 96. Although the American economic system is private in character, economists usually describe the nation as having a mixed economy. What two elements coexist in this mixture?
- a. corporate sponsorship and sole proprietorship
- b. partnerships and corporations
- c. private enterprise and governmental participation
- d. public works and private enterprise

_____ 97. Why would socialism be an especially attractive philosophy for a developing nation?
- a. The depressed economy of a developing nation naturally rebounds when placed under foreign control and ownership, reducing investments internationally while stimulating growth.
- b. By limiting the layers of bureaucracy, socialist countries minimize decision making and improve individual initiative, which can boost a developing nation's growth.
- c. Socialism appeals to leaders who want to mobilize an entire nation behind a single program of industrial growth, channeling investment into the parts of the economy that are most essential.
- d. With a tradition of locally controlled, large-scale industry, developing nations are attracted to the small-scale, government-owned industry representative of socialism.

_____ 98. Karl Marx predicted that workers in different countries would revolt and embrace communism. Which of the following did he NOT anticipate?
- a. Communism would be hastened by revolution.
- b. Economic growth and productivity would decline.
- c. Social classes would vanish and all property would be communal.
- d. People's national loyalties and sentiments would intensify.

_____ 99. Mao Zedong's patriotic movement appealed to
- a. the intellectual elite.
- b. prosperous businessmen.
- c. the Chinese peasantry.
- d. the United States.

_____ 100. When did the Soviet Union cease to exist?
- a. in 1989, when the Baltic Soviet states of Lithuania, Latvia, and Estonia sought independence
- b. by mid-1990, when the republics of Russia, Ukraine, and Byelorussia declared independence from the Soviet central authority
- c. in mid-1991, when an attempted coup by Communist Party leaders failed
- d. in late 1991, when Mikhail Gorbachev resigned as president of the Soviet Union

Key Terms

Act of admission A congressional act admitting a new State to the Union

Albany Plan of Union Plan proposed by Benjamin Franklin in 1754 that aimed to unite the 13 colonies for trade, military, and other purposes; the plan was turned down by the colonies and the Crown.

Amendment A change in, or addition to, a constitution or law

Anti-Federalists Those persons who opposed the ratification of the Constitution in 1787–1788

Articles Numbered sections of a document. The unamended Constitution is divided into seven articles

Authoritarian A form of government in which those in power hold absolute and unchangeable authority over the people; all dictatorships are authoritarian.

Bicameral An adjective describing a legislative body composed of two chambers

Block grant One type of federal grants-in-aid for some particular but broadly defined area of public policy

Boycott Refusal to buy or sell certain products or services

Cabinet Presidential advisory body, traditionally made up of the heads of the executive departments and other officers

Categorical grant One type of federal grants-in-aid; made for some specific, closely defined purpose

Charter A city's basic law, its constitution; a written grant of authority from the king

Checks and balances System of overlapping the powers of the legislative, executive, and judicial branches to permit each branch to check the actions of the others

Compromise An adjustment of opposing principles or systems by modifying some aspect of each

Concurrent powers Those powers that both the National Government and the States possess and exercise

Constitutionalism Basic principle that government and those who govern must obey the law; the rule of law

Delegate Representative; lawmaker who views him or herself as the agent of those who elected him or her and votes accordingly, regardless of his or her personal opinions

Delegated powers Those powers, expressed, implied, or inherent, granted to the National Government by the Constitution

Electoral college Group of persons chosen in each State and the District of Columbia every four years who make a formal selection of the President and Vice President

Enabling act A congressional act directing the people of a United States territory to frame a proposed State constitution as a step toward admission to the Union

Exclusive powers Those powers that can be exercised by the National Government alone

Executive agreement A pact made by the President directly with the head of a foreign state; a binding international agreement with the force of law but which (unlike a treaty) does not require Senate consent

Executive power The power to execute, enforce, and administer law

Expressed powers Those delegated powers of the National Government that are spelled out, expressly, in the Constitution; also called the "enumerated powers"

Extradition The legal process by which a fugitive from justice from a State is returned to that State

Federalism A system of government in which a written constitution divides power between a central, or national, government and several regional governments

Federalists Those persons who supported the ratification of the Constitution in 1787–1788

Formal amendment Change or addition that becomes part of the written language of the Constitution itself through one of four methods set forth in the Constitution

Framers Group of delegates who drafted the United States Constitution at the Philadelphia Convention in 1787

Free enterprise system An economic system characterized by private or corporate ownership of capital goods; investments that are determined by private decision rather than by state control and are determined in a free market

Full Faith and Credit Clause Constitution's requirement that each State accept the public acts, records, and judicial proceedings of every other State

Government The institution through which a society makes and enforces its public policies

Grants-in-aid program Grants of federal money or other resources to States, cities, counties, and other local units

Implied powers Those delegated powers of the National Government that are suggested by the expressed powers; those "necessary and proper" to carry out the expressed powers

Informal amendment A change made in the Constitution not by actual written amendment but by the experience of government, including (1) the passage of laws by Congress; (2) actions taken by the President; (3) Supreme Court decisions; (4) the activities of political parties; and (5) custom

Inherent powers Powers delegated to the National Government because it is the government of a sovereign state within the world community

Interstate compact Formal agreement entered into with the consent of Congress, between or among States, or between a State and a foreign state

Judicial power The power to interpret laws, to determine their meanings, and to settle disputes within the society

Judicial review The power of a court to determine the Constitutionality of a government action

Law of supply and demand A law that states that when supplies of goods and services become plentiful, prices tend to drop; when supplies become scarce, prices tend to rise.

Legislative power The power to make a law and to frame public policies

Limited government Basic principle of American government that states that government is restricted in what it may do and that each individual has rights that government cannot take away

Mixed economy An economy in which private enterprise exists in combination with a considerable amount of government regulation and promotion

Popular sovereignty Basic principle of the American system of government that asserts that the people are the source of any and all governmental power and that government can exist only with the consent of the governed

Preamble Introduction

Presiding officer Chair

Privileges and Immunities Clause Constitution's stipulations (Article IV, Section 2) that all citizens are entitled to certain "privileges and immunities," regardless of their State of residence; no State can draw unreasonable distinctions between its own residents and those persons who happen to live in other States

Project grant One type of federal grants-in-aid; made for specific projects to States, localities, and private agencies who apply for them

Proprietary Organized by a proprietor (a person to whom the king had made a grant of land)

Public policy All of the goals a government sets and the various courses of action it pursues as it attempts to realize these goals

Quorum Least number of members who must be present for a legislative body to conduct business; majority

Ratification Formal approval; final consent to the effectiveness of a constitution, constitutional amendment, or treaty

Repeal Recall

Representative government System of government in which public policies are made by officials selected by the voters and held accountable in periodic elections

Reserved powers Those powers that the Constitution does not grant to the National Government and does not, at the same time, deny to the States

Revenue sharing Form of federal monetary aid under which Congress gave a share of federal tax revenue, with virtually no restrictions, to the States, cities, counties, and townships

Rule of law Concept that holds that government and its officers are always subject to the law

Senatorial courtesy Custom that the Senate will not approve a presidential appointment opposed by a majority party senator from the State in which the appointee would serve

Separation of powers Basic principle of American system of government, that states that the executive, legislative, and judicial powers are divided among three independent and coequal branches of government

Sovereign Having supreme power within its own territory; neither subordinate nor responsible to any other authority

State A body of people living in a defined territory who have a government with the power to make and enforce law without the consent of any higher authority

Totalitarian A government that exercises dictatorial (authoritarian) power over nearly every aspect of human affairs

Treaty A formal agreement between two or more sovereign states

Unconstitutional Contrary to constitutional provision and so illegal, null and void, of no force and effect

Unicameral An adjective describing a legislative body with one chamber

Veto Chief executive's power to reject a bill passed by a legislature; literally (Latin), "I forbid"

Forms of Government

autocracy A form of government in which a single person holds unlimited political power

confederation A joining of several groups for a common purpose

democracy A form of government in which the supreme authority rests with the people

dictatorship A form of government in which the leader has absolute power and authority

federal government A form of government in which powers are divided between a central government and several local governments

oligarchy A form of government in which the power to rule is held by a small, usually self-appointed elite

parliamentary government A form of government in which the executive branch is made up of the prime minister, or premier, and that official's cabinet

presidential government A form of government in which the executive and legislative branches of government are separate, independent, and coequal

unitary government A centralized system in which all powers of government belong to a single, central agency

© Pearson Education, Inc.

Landmark English Documents

Magna Carta (1215) Signed by King John; included protections against the absolute power of the king, such as the right to trial by jury and due process of law—protection against the arbitrary taking of life, liberty, and property

Petition of Right (1628) Limited the king's power and challenged the idea of the divine right of kings, declaring that even a monarch must obey the law of the land

English Bill of Rights (1689) Drawn up by Parliament after the Glorious Revolution to prevent the abuse of power by future monarchs; included the right to a free trial, freedom from excessive bail, and freedom from cruel and unusual punishment

Plans and Compromises at the Constitutional Convention

Commerce and Slave Trade Compromise Agreement during the Constitutional Convention protecting slave holders; denied Congress the power to tax the export of goods from any State, and, for 20 years, the power to act on the slave trade

Connecticut Compromise Agreement during the Constitutional Convention that Congress should be composed of a Senate, in which States would be represented equally, and a House, in which the number of representatives would be based on a State's population

New Jersey Plan Plan presented as an alternative to the Virginia Plan at the Constitutional Convention; called for a unicameral legislature in which each State would be equally represented

Three-Fifths Compromise Agreement at the Constitutional Convention to count a slave as three-fifths of a person when determining the population of a State

Virginia Plan Plan presented by delegates from Virginia at the Constitutional Convention; called for a three-branch government with a bicameral legislature in which each State's membership would be determined by its population or its financial support for the central government

Key People

Franklin, Benjamin Delegate of the Second Continental Congress, public servant, commissioner to France during the War for Independence, and member of the Constitutional Convention

Hamilton, Alexander Contributor to *The Federalist* and framer of the Constitution

Hancock, John President of the Second Continental Congress

Hobbes, Thomas English philosopher who argued that government was necessary for the prosperity and safety of all

Jefferson, Thomas Primary author of the Declaration of Independence; delegate to Second Continental Congress; third President of the United States

Locke, John English thinker whose theories on government provided inspiration for the Declaration of Independence

Madison, James Contributor to the Constitution; primary author of the Virginia Plan; contributor to *The Federalist*; fourth President of the United States

Marshall, John Chief Justice of the Supreme Court from 1801 to 1835; set precedents that established important powers of the federal courts

Washington, George Commander of the Revolutionary army; president of the Constitutional Convention; first President of the United States

Basic Elements of the State

Population	A state must have people.
Territory	A state must have land, with known and recognized boundaries.
Sovereignty	A state has supreme and absolute power within its own territory and decides its own foreign and domestic policies. It is neither subordinate nor responsible to any other authority.
Government	A state is politically organized.

Key Events

Date	Event	Significance
1643	New England Confederation	Early cooperation between colonies for common defense against the Native Americans; dissolved in 1684
1754	Albany Plan of Union	Devised by Benjamin Franklin to provide for the defense of the American colonies and to discuss trade; included an annual congress of delegates from each colony
1760	George III Crowned	Britain began to deal more firmly with the colonies, imposing taxes that colonists considered objectionable.
1765	Stamp Act Congress	The first time a significant number of colonies joined to oppose the British government
1770	Boston Massacre	Incident in which British soldiers killed five colonists
1773	Boston Tea Party	Colonial protest of British control of the tea trade
1774	First Continental Congress	Sent a Declaration of Rights protesting Britain's colonial policies to George III
1775	Second Continental Congress	First national government until the Articles of Confederation went into effect in 1781
1776	Declaration of Independence	Statement, issued by the Second Continental Congress, that explained why the American colonies were seeking independence from Britain
1781	Articles of Confederation	Plan of government under which the United States operated until its replacement by the Constitution
1787	Constitutional Convention	Meeting of delegates from 12 states who wrote the United States Constitution
1791	Bill of Rights	First ten Amendments to the Constitution; listing of basic rights held by the American people

The Structure of Government

There are only two basic levels in the federal system: the National Government and the State governments. Each level of government has specific powers reserved for it.

National Government

The national government has the power to coin money, regulate interstate and foreign trade, recruit and maintain armed forces, declare war, govern United States territories and admit new States, and conduct foreign relations.

State Government

The state governments have the power to regulate trade and business within the State, establish public schools, pass license requirements for professionals, regulate alcoholic beverages, conduct elections, and establish local governments.

Articles of the Constitution

Section	Subject
Preamble	States the purpose of the Constitution
Article I	Legislative branch
Article II	Executive branch
Article III	Judicial branch
Article IV	Relations among the States
Article V	Amending the Constitution
Article VI	National debts, supremacy of national law, and oaths of office
Article VII	Ratifying the Constitution

Key Terms

Bankruptcy The legal proceeding by which a bankrupt person's assets are distributed among those to whom he or she owes debts

Bipartisan Supported by two parties

Blanket primary A voting process in which voters receive a long ballot containing the names of all contenders, regardless of party, and can vote however they choose

Closed primary A party nominating election in which only declared party members can vote

Coalition A temporary alliance of several groups who come together to form a working majority and so to control a government

Coattail effect The effect of a strong candidate running for an office at the top of a ballot helping to attract voters to other candidates on the party's ticket

Consensus General agreement among various groups on fundamental matters; broad agreement on public questions

Division of powers Basic principle of federalism; the constitutional provisions by which governmental powers are divided on a geographic basis (in the United States, between the National Government and the States)

Economic protest parties Parties rooted in poor economic times, lacking a clear ideological base, dissatisfied with current conditions and demanding better times

Electorate All of the people entitled to vote in a given election

Gender gap Measurable differences between the partisan choices of men and women today

General election The regularly scheduled election at which voters make a final selection of officeholders

Gerrymandering The drawing of electoral district lines to the advantage of a party or group

Grass roots Of or from the people; the average voters

Hard money Campaign money that is subject to regulations by the Federal Election Committee

Ideological parties Parties based on a particular set of beliefs, with a comprehensive view of social, economic, and political matters

Incumbent The current officeholder

Independents People who have no party affiliation

Inherent powers Powers delegated to the National Government because it is the government of a sovereign state within the world community

Injunction A court order that forces or limits the performance of some act by a private individual or by a public official

Interest group Private organizations whose members share certain views and work to shape public policy

Labor union An organization of workers who share the same type of job or work in the same industry and press for government policies that will benefit the organization's members

Lobbying Activities by which group pressures are brought to bear on legislators, the legislative process, and all aspects of the public policy making process

Major parties In American politics, the Republican and the Democratic parties

Mandate The instructions or commands a constituency gives to its elected officials

Minor party One of the political parties not widely supported

Multiparty A system in which several major and many lesser parties exist, and seriously compete for, and actually win, public offices

Nonpartisan election Elections in which candidates are not identified by party labels

Off-year election Congressional election that occurs between presidential election years

One-party system A political system in which only one party exists

Open primary A party-nominating election in which any qualified voter can take part

Opinion leader Any person who, for any reason, has an unusually strong influence on the view of others

Partisanship Government action based on firm allegiance to a political party

Party in power In American politics, the party in power is the party that controls the executive branch of government—e.g. the presidency at the national level or the governorship at the State level

Pluralistic society A society that consists of several distinct cultures and groups

Plurality In an election, the number of votes that the leading candidate obtains over the next highest candidate

Political action committee The political extension of special-interest groups that have a major stake in public policy

Political efficacy One's own influence on or effectiveness in politics

Political party A group of persons who seek to control government through winning elections and holding public office

Political socialization The process by which people gain their political attitudes and opinions

Poll book List of all registered voters in each precinct

Poll tax A special tax, demanded by the States as a condition of voting

Polling place The place where the voters who live in a certain precinct go to vote

Preclearance Mandated by the Voting Rights Act of 1965; the prior approval by the Justice Department of changes to or new election laws by certain States

Propaganda A technique of persuasion aimed at influencing individual or group behaviors to create a particular belief, regardless of its validity

Public affairs Those events and issues that concern the people at large—e.g., politics, public issues, and the making of public policies

Public agenda The public issues on which the people's attention is focused

Public-interest group An interest group that seeks to institute certain public policies of benefit to all or most people in this country regardless of whether they belong to or support that organization

Public opinion The complex collection of the opinions of many different people; the sum of all their views

Public opinion poll Device that attempts to collect information by asking people questions

Public policy All of the goals a government sets and the various courses of action it pursues as it attempts to realize these goals

Purge The process of reviewing lists of registered voters and removing the names of those no longer eligible to vote; a purification

Quota sample A sample deliberately constructed to reflect several of the major characteristics of a given population

Random sample A certain number of randomly selected people who live in a certain number of randomly selected places

Registration A procedure of voter identification intended to prevent fraudulent voting

Runoff primary A primary in which the top two vote-getters in the first direct primary face one another

Sample A representative slice of the public

Sectionalism A narrow-minded concern for, or devotion to, the interests of one section of a country

Single-interest group Political action committee that concentrates its efforts exclusively on one issue

Single-issue parties Parties that concentrate on only one public policy matter

Single-member district Electoral district from which one person is chosen by the voters for each elected office

Soft money Money given to State and local party organizations for voting-related activities

Splinter parties Parties that have split away from one of the major parties

Split-ticket voting Voting for candidates of different parties for different offices in the same election

Straight-ticket voting The practice of voting for candidates of only one party in an election

Straw vote Polls that seek to read the public's mind simply by asking the same question of a large number of people

Strict constructionist One who argues a narrow interpretation of the Constitution's provisions, in particular those granting powers to the Federal Government

Subsidy A grant of money, usually from a government

Suffrage The right to vote

Trade association Interest groups within the business community

Transient Person living in a State for only a short time, without legal residence

Two-party system A political system dominated by two major parties

Ward A unit into which cites are often divided for the election of city council members

Major and Minor Political Parties

Type	Example	Description
Major	Democratic	Election-oriented party
Major	Republican	Election-oriented party
Minor: Ideological Party	Libertarian	Emphasizes individualism and calls for doing away with most of government's present functions and programs
Minor: Ideological Party	Socialist	Emphasizes socialist ideals of government
Minor: Single-Issue Party	Free Soil	Opposed the spread of slavery (1840s and 1850s)
Minor: Single-Issue Party	Right to Life	Opposes abortion
Minor: Economic Protest Party	Greenback	Appealed to struggling farmers by calling for the free coinage of silver, federal regulation of the railroads, an income tax, and labor legislation (1876–1884)
Minor: Economic Protest Party	Populist	Demanded public ownership of railroads, and telephone and telegraph companies, lower tariffs, and the adoption of the initiative and referendum (1890s)
Minor: Splinter Party	"Bull Moose" Progressive	Formed around the personality of Theodore Roosevelt in the election of 1912
Minor	Green	Began as a single-issue party; now focuses on universal health care, gay and lesbian rights, restraints on corporate power, campaign finance reform, and opposition to global free trade as well as environmental protection

Evolution of the Right to Vote

Date	Significance
1789	With the Constitution, the right to vote was extended to white male property owners.
Early 1800s	The elimination of religious qualifications, property ownership, and tax payment qualifications granted almost all white adult males the right to vote in every State by mid-century.
1870	The Fifteenth Amendment was intended to protect any citizen from being denied the right to vote because of race or color. Still, for nearly a century, African Americans were systematically prevented from voting.
1920	The Nineteenth Amendment prohibited the denial of the right to vote because of gender.
1960s	With the passage and vigorous enforcement of a number of civil rights acts, particularly the Voting Rights Act of 1965 and its later extensions, voting equality finally became a fact in polling booths throughout the country.
1971	The Twenty-Sixth Amendment provided that no State can set the minimum age for voting at more than 18 years of age.

How Elections Work

Step One: Nomination The naming of those who will seek office; there are five ways in which nominations are made in the United States.

- **self-announcement** A person who wants to run for office announces that fact
- **caucus** A group of like-minded people meet to select the candidates they will support in an upcoming election
- **convention** Nominees are chosen from delegates selected by a series of conventions, from local to national
- **direct primary** An intra-party election held to pick that party's candidates for the general election
- **petition** Candidates for public office are nominated by means of petitions signed by a required number of qualified voters in the election district

Step Two: Raising Money Running for public office costs money, often a lot of it. Parties and their candidates draw their money from two basic sources—contributors and the public treasury.

Step Three: Voting for Candidates

- **absentee voting** Voting by those unable to get to their regular polling places on election day
- **precincts** A voting district supervised by an election board that makes certain only qualified voters cast ballots in the precinct
- **casting ballots** The method by which a voter registers a choice in an election

Functions of Political Parties

Nominate candidates	The major function of political parties is to select candidates and present them to the voters.
Inform and activate supporters	Political parties campaign for candidates, take stands on issues, and criticize opponents.
Act as bonding agents	Political parties ensure good performance of its candidates and officeholders.
Govern	Firm allegiance to a political party is basis for government action.
Act as watchdog	Political parties check the operations of the other parties.

The Nominating Process

Self-announcement	A person announces a bid for office.
Caucus/convention	Party delegates nominate candidates.
Direct primary	An intra-party election is held to pick its candidates for the general election.
Petition	Candidates are nominated by petitions signed by a required number of qualified voters in the election district.

Key Terms

Acquit Find not guilty of a charge

Adjourn Suspend, as in a session of Congress

Apportion Distribute, as in seats in a legislative body

Appropriate Assign to a particular issue

At-large election Election of an officeholder by the voters of an entire governmental unit rather than by the voters of a district or subdivision

Bill A proposed law presented to a legislative body for consideration

Bipartisan Supported by two parties

Censure Issue a formal condemnation

Cloture Procedure that may be used to limit or end floor debate in a legislative body

Commerce power Exclusive power of Congress to regulate interstate and foreign trade

Committee chairman Member who heads a standing committee in a legislative body

Committee of the Whole A committee that consists of an entire legislative body; used for a procedure in which a legislative body expedites its business by resolving itself into a committee of itself

Concurrent resolution A statement of position on an issue used by the House and Senate acting jointly; does not have the force of law and does not require the President's signature

Conference committee Temporary joint committee created to reconcile any differences between the two houses' versions of a bill

Consensus General agreement among various groups on fundamental matters; broad agreement on public questions

Constituency The people and interests that an elected official represents

Continuous body Governing unit whose seats are never all up for election at the same time

Copyright The exclusive, legal right of a person to reproduce, publish, and sell his or her own literary, musical, or artistic creations

Deficit financing Practice of funding government by borrowing to make up the difference between government spending and revenue

Direct tax A tax that must be paid by the person on whom it is levied

Discharge petition A procedure enabling members to force a bill that has been pigeonholed in committee onto the floor for consideration

Doctrine Principle or fundamental policy

Eminent domain Power of a government to take private property for public use

Engross To print a bill in its final form

Filibuster Various tactics aimed at defeating a bill in a legislative body by preventing a final vote; associated with the U.S. Senate

Floor leaders Members of the House and Senate picked by their parties to carry out party decisions and steer legislative action to meet party goals

Franking privilege Benefit allowing member of Congress to mail letters and other materials postage-free

Impeach To bring formal charges against a public official; the House of Representatives has the sole power to impeach civil officers of the United States

Indirect tax A tax levied on one party but passed on to another for payment

Joint committee Legislative committee composed of members of both houses

Joint resolution A proposal for action that has the force of law when passed; usually deals with special circumstances or temporary matters

Legal tender Any kind of money that a creditor must, by law, accept in payment for debts

Liberal constructionist One who argues a broad interpretation of the provisions of the Constitution, particularly those granting powers to the Federal Government

Naturalization The legal process by which citizens of one country become citizens of another

Necessary and Proper Clause Constitutional clause that gives Congress the power to make all laws "necessary and proper" for executing its powers

Off-year election Congressional election that occurs between presidential election years

Oversight function Review by legislative committees of the policies and programs of the executive branch

Partisan Lawmaker who owes his or her first allegiance to his or her political party and votes according to the party line

Party caucus A closed meeting of a party's House or Senate members; also called a party conference

Patent A license issued to an inventor granting the exclusive right to manufacture, use, or sell his or her invention for a limited period of time

Perjury The act of lying under oath

Pocket veto Type of veto a chief executive may use after a legislature has adjourned; when the chief executive does not sign or reject a bill within the time allowed to do so

Politico Lawmaker who attempts to balance the basic elements of the trustee, delegate, and partisan roles

President of the Senate The presiding officer of a senate; in Congress, the Vice President of the United States; in a State's legislature, either the lieutenant governor or a senator

President *pro tempore* The member of the United States Senate, or of the upper house of a State's legislature, chosen to preside in the absence of the president of the Senate

Prorogue Adjourn, as in a legislative session

Public debt All of the money borrowed by the government and not yet repaid plus the accrued interest on that money; also called the national debt or federal debt

Reapportion Redistribute, as in seats in a legislative body

Resolution A measure relating to the business of either house or expressing an opinion; does not have the force of law and does not require the President's signature

Rider Unpopular provision added to an important bill certain to pass so that it will "ride" through the legislative process

Select committee Legislative committee created for a limited time and for some specific purpose; also known as a special committee

Seniority rule Unwritten rule in both houses of Congress reserving the top posts in each chamber, particularly committee chairs, for members with the longest records of service

Speaker of the House The presiding officer of the House of Representatives, chosen by and from the majority party in the House

Special session An extraordinary session of a legislative body, called to deal with an emergency situation

Standing committee Permanent committee in a legislative body to which bills in a specified subject-matter area are referred

Subcommittee Division of existing committee that is formed to address specific issues

Subpoena An order for a person to appear and to produce documents or other requested materials

Successor A person who inherits a title or office

Tax A charge levied by government on persons or property to meet public needs

Trustee Lawmaker who votes based on his or her conscience and judgment, not the views of his or her constituents

Whips Assistants to the floor leaders in the House and Senate, responsible for monitoring and marshaling votes

The Structure of Congress

The Framers of the Constitution created a Congress with two bodies: a small Senate and a much larger House of Representatives. Each Congress since 1789 has met for a term of two years, divided into two one-year sessions.

- **The Senate** The Senate is composed of 100 members, two Senators from each State. Senators serve six-year terms, must be at least 30 years of age, must have been a citizen of the United States for at least nine years, and must be an inhabitant of the State from which he or she is elected.

- **The House of Representatives** The total number of seats in the House of Representatives is distributed among States on the basis of population, reapportioned after each decennial census. A member of the House must be at least 25, a citizen of the United States for at least seven years, and an inhabitant of the State from which he or she is elected. A member is elected for a term of two years.

The Powers of Congress

The Constitution grants Congress a number of specific powers:

- **Expressed Powers** Expressed powers of Congress are the power to tax, to regulate interstate and foreign trade, to borrow money, to coin money and regulate currency, to declare war, to regulate naturalization, to establish post offices, to grant patents and copyrights, to create courts inferior to the Supreme Court, to define and punish crimes at sea and violations of international law, and to make all laws necessary and proper to the execution of any of the other expressed powers.

- **Implied Powers** The implied powers of Congress are derived from the expressed powers. Some of the implied powers of Congress are: the power to regulate the sale of some commodities and outlaw others, to establish the

Federal Reserve System, to draft Americans into the military, to establish a minimum wage, and to ban discrimination in workplaces and public facilities.

- **Inherent Powers** The inherent powers belong to the National Government because it is the government of a sovereign state within the world community. They are few in number. The major ones include: the power to regulate immigration, to deport undocumented aliens, to acquire territory, to give diplomatic recognition to other states, and to protect the nation against rebellion or other attempts to overthrow the government.

Qualifications to Hold Congressional Office

House	Senate
at least 25 years old	at least 30 years old
a citizen of the United States for at least seven years	a citizen of the United States for at least nine years
an inhabitant of the State from which he or she is elected	an inhabitant of the State from which he or she is elected

Major Differences between the Houses of Congress

House	Senate
435 members	100 members
2-year term	6-year term
elected from districts within States	elected from entire State
strict rules; limited debate	flexible rules; nearly unlimited debate
most work in done in committees, not on the floor	work is split more evenly between committees and the floor
no power over treaties and presidential appointments	approves or rejects treaties and presidential appointments

Key Congressional Powers

Expressed

Peacetime Powers

- to establish and collect taxes, duties, and excises
- to borrow money
- to regulate foreign and interstate commerce
- to create naturalization laws; to create bankruptcy laws
- to coin money and regulate its value; to regulate weights and measures
- to punish counterfeiters of federal money and securities
- to establish post offices
- to grant patents and copyrights
- to create courts inferior to the Supreme Court
- to define and punish crimes at sea and violations of international law
- to exercise exclusive jurisdiction over the District of Columbia and other federal properties
- to make all laws necessary and proper to the execution of any of the other expressed powers

Wartime Powers

- to declare war; to make laws regarding captures on land and water
- to raise and support armies
- to provide and maintain a navy
- to make laws governing land and naval forces
- to provided for summoning the militia to execute federal laws, suppress uprisings, and repel invasions
- to provide for organizing, arming, and disciplining the militia and governing it when in the service of the Union

Implied

- to punish tax evaders
- to regulate the sale of some commodities and outlaw the use of others
- to require States to meet certain conditions to qualify for federal funding
- to establish the Federal Reserve System of banks
- to regulate and limit immigration
- to draft Americans into the military
- to establish a minimum wage
- to ban discrimination in workplace and public facilities
- to pass laws protecting the disabled
- to regulate banking
- to prohibit mail fraud and obstruction of the mails
- to bar the shipping of certain items through the mail

The Impeachment Process

Step 1	House Judiciary Committee debates charges against the accused and votes on whether to send articles of impeachment to the full House. A simple majority vote is needed to start the process.
Step 2	Acting much like a grand jury, the House considers the charge(s) brought by the Judiciary Committee. It can subpoena witnesses and evidence. It hears and debates arguments.
Step 3	House votes on each article. If any article is approved by a majority vote, the official is impeached, which is similar to being indicted. House sends article(s) of impeachment to the Senate.
Step 4	Trial is held in the Senate, with the Chief Justice of the United States presiding. Senators act as jurors, but may also engage in questioning. Selected House members act as prosecutors.
Step 5	Senators hear testimony and evidence. House prosecutors and lawyers for both sides present their cases. Additional witnesses may be called. Senators may also vote to curb testimony.
Step 6	Senate debates the article, publicly or privately. It does not have to render a verdict. It could vote to drop the case or censure the official. A two-thirds vote is required for conviction.

Types of Bills and Resolutions

Bill	A proposed law or draft of a law. A public bill applies to the entire nation. A private bill applies only to certain people or places.
Joint resolution	A proposal for action that has the force of law when passed. It usually deals with special circumstances or temporary matters.
Concurrent resolution	A statement of position on an issue used by the House and Senate acting jointly. It does not have the force of law and it does not require the President's signature.
Resolution	A measure relating to the business of either house or expression an opinion on a matter that does not have the force of law. It does not require the President's signature.

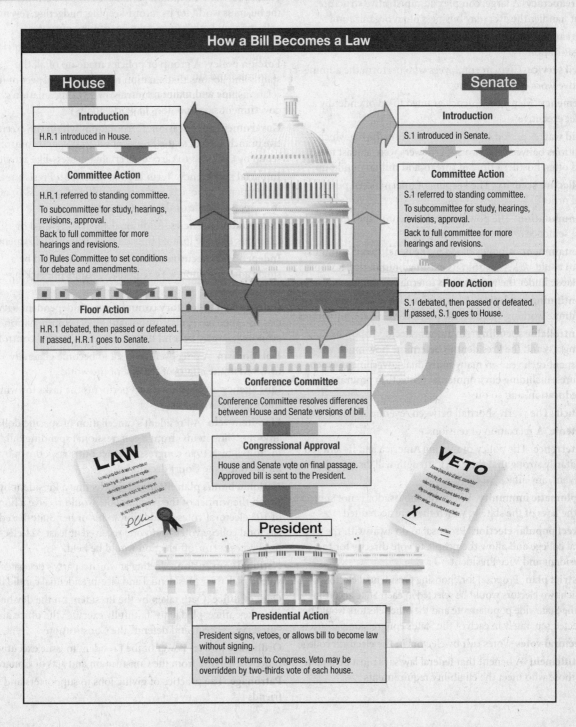

How a Bill Becomes a Law

House

Introduction
H.R.1 introduced in House.

Committee Action
H.R.1 referred to standing committee.
To subcommittee for study, hearings, revisions, approval.
Back to full committee for more hearings and revisions.
To Rules Committee to set conditions for debate and amendments.

Floor Action
H.R.1 debated, then passed or defeated.
If passed, H.R.1 goes to Senate.

Senate

Introduction
S.1 introduced in Senate.

Committee Action
S.1 referred to standing committee.
To subcommittee for study, hearings, revisions, approval.
Back to full committee for more hearings and revisions.

Floor Action
S.1 debated, then passed or defeated.
If passed, S.1 goes to House.

Conference Committee
Conference Committee resolves differences between House and Senate versions of bill.

Congressional Approval
House and Senate vote on final passage.
Approved bill is sent to the President.

LAW

VETO

President

Presidential Action
President signs, vetoes, or allows bill to become law without signing.
Vetoed bill returns to Congress. Veto may be overridden by two-thirds vote of each house.

Key Terms

Administration The officials in the executive branch of a government and their policies and principles

Ambassador An official representative of the United States, appointed by the President to represent the nation in matters of diplomacy

Amnesty A blanket pardon offered to a group of law violators

Attorney General The head of the Department of Justice

Bureaucracy A large, complex administrative structure that handles the everyday business of an organization

Bureaucrat A person who works for a bureaucratic organization

Civil service Civilian employees who perform the administrative work of government

Clemency Mercy or leniency granted to an offender by a chief executive

Cold war A period of more than 40 years during which relations between the two superpowers were at least tense and often hostile; a time of threats and military build up

Collective security The keeping of international peace and order

Commutation The power to reduce (commute) the length of a sentence or fine for a crime

Containment A policy based in the belief that if communism could be kept within its existing boundaries, it would collapse under the weight of its internal weaknesses

Continuing resolution A measure which allows agencies to continue working based on the previous year's appropriations

Controllable spending An amount decided upon by Congress and the President to determine how much will be spent each year on many individual government expenditures, including environmental protection programs, aid to education, and so on

Deficit The yearly shortfall between revenue and spending

Détente A relaxation of tensions

Deterrence The policy of making America and its allies so militarily strong that their very strength will discourage, or prevent, any attack.

Diplomatic immunity When an ambassador is not subject to the laws of the state to which they are accredited

Direct popular election Proposal to do away with the electoral college and allow the people to vote directly for the President and Vice President

District plan Proposal for choosing presidential electors by which two electors would be selected in each State according to the Statewide popular vote and the other electors would be selected separately in each of the State's congressional districts

Electoral votes Votes cast by electors in the electoral college

Entitlement A benefit that federal law says must be paid to all those who meet the eligibility requirements

Executive Article Article II of the Constitution; establishes the presidency and gives the executive power of the Federal Government to the President

Executive order Directive, rule, or regulation issued by a chief executive or subordinates, based upon constitutional or statutory authority and having the force of law

Federal budget A detailed financial document containing estimates of federal income and spending during the coming fiscal year

Fiscal year The 12-month period used by a government and the business world for its record-keeping, budgeting, revenue-collecting, and other financial management purposes

Foreign aid Economic and military aid to other countries

Foreign policy A group of policies made up of all the stands and actions that a nation takes in every aspect of its relationships with other countries; everything a nation's government says and does in world affairs

Government corporation Corporations within the executive branch subject to the President's direction and control, set up by Congress to carry out certain business-like activities

Imperial presidency Term used to describe a President as an "emperor" who acts without consulting Congress or acts in secrecy to evade or deceive Congress

Independent agencies Additional agencies created by Congress that are located outside the Cabinet departments

Independent executive agencies Agencies headed by a single administrator, with regional subunits but lacking Cabinet status

Independent regulatory commissions Independent agencies designed to regulate important aspects of the nation's economy; largely beyond the reach of presidential control

Isolationism A purposeful refusal to become generally involved in the affairs of the rest of the world

Line agency An agency which performs the tasks for which the organization exists

Line-item veto A President's cancellation of specific dollar amounts (line items) from a congressional spending bill; instituted by a 1996 congressional act but struck down by a 1998 Supreme Court decision

National bonus plan Proposal for electing a President by which the winner of the popular vote would receive a bonus of 102 electoral votes in addition to his or her State-based electoral college votes. If no one received at least 321 electoral votes, a run-off election would be held.

National convention Meeting at which a party's delegates vote to pick their presidential and vice-presidential candidates

Oath of office Oath taken by the President on the day he or she takes office; pledge to "faithfully execute" the office and "preserve, protect, and defend" the Constitution

Ordinance power Power of the President to issue executive orders; originates from the Constitution and acts of Congress

Patronage The practice of giving jobs to supporters and friends

Payroll tax A tax imposed on nearly all employers and their employees and on self-employed persons; the amounts owed by employees withheld from their paychecks

Persona non grata An unwelcome person; used to describe recalled diplomatic officials

Platform A political party's formal statement of basic principles, stands on major issues, and objectives

Political asylum The provision of a safe haven for those persecuted

Presidential elector A person elected by the voters to represent them in making a formal selection of the Vice President and President

Presidential primary An election in which a party's voters (1) choose State party organizations' delegates to their party's national convention, and/or (2) express a preference for their party's presidential nomination

Presidential succession Scheme by which a presidential vacancy is filled

Presidential Succession Act of 1947 Law specifying the order of presidential succession following the Vice President

Progressive tax A type of tax proportionate to income

Proportional plan Proposal by which each presidential candidate would receive the same share of a State's electoral vote as he or she received in the State's popular vote

Proportional representation rule Rule applied in Democratic primaries whereby any candidate who wins at least 15 percent of the votes gets the number of State Democratic convention delegates based on his or her share of that primary vote

Public debt All of the money borrowed by the government and not yet repaid, plus the accrued interest on that money; also called the national debt or federal debt

Quasi-judicial Having to do with powers that are to some extent judicial

Quasi-legislative Having to do with powers that are to some extent legislative

Recognition The exclusive power of a President to recognize (establish formal diplomatic relations with) foreign states

Regional security alliances Treaties in which the United States and other countries involved have agreed to take collective action to meet aggression in a particular part of the world

Register A record or list of names, often kept by an official appointed to do so

Regressive tax A tax levied at a flat rate, without regard to the level of a taxpayer's income or ability to pay

Reprieve An official postponement of the execution of a sentence

Right of legation The right to send and receive diplomatic representatives

Secretary An official in charge of a department of government

Spoils system The practice of giving offices and other favors of government to political supporters and friends

Staff agency An agency that supports the chief executive and other administrators by offering advice and other assistance in the management of the organization

Surplus More income than spending

Tax return A declaration of taxable income and of the exemptions and deductions claimed

Treaty A formal agreement between two or more sovereign states

UN Security Council A fifteen-member panel that bears the UN's major responsibility for maintaining international peace

Uncontrollable spending Spending that Congress and the President have no power to change directly

Winner-take-all An almost obsolete system whereby a presidential aspirant who won the preference vote in a primary automatically won all the delegates chosen in the primary

The President's Roles

chief administrator Term for the President as head of the administration of the Federal Government

chief citizen Term for the President as the representative of the people, working for and representing the public interest

chief diplomat Term for the President as the main architect of foreign policy and spokesperson to other countries

chief executive Term for the President as vested with the executive power of the United States

chief legislator Term for the President as architect of public policy and the one who sets the agenda for Congress

chief of party Term for the President as the leader of his or her political party

chief of state Term for the President as the ceremonial head of the United States, the symbol of all the people of the nation

commander in chief Term for the President as commander of the nation's armed forces

Presidential Powers

Executive Powers As chief executive, the President executes the provisions of federal law. The President may issue executive orders, appoint most of the top-ranking officers of the Federal Government, and remove people from office.

Diplomatic and Military Powers The President has the power to make treaties and executive agreements, to recognize another sovereign state, to command the nation's armed forces, and to ration food and gasoline, control wages and prices, and seize and operate private industries in a time of war.

Legislative and Judicial Powers The President has the power to recommend legislation to Congress, to veto legislation, and to call Congress into special session. In addition, the President may postpone executions and pardon criminals guilty of federal offenses.

Structure of the Executive Branch

Executive Office of the President The EOP is a complex organization of several separate agencies staffed by most of the President's closest advisors and assistants, including the White House Office, the National Security Council, the Office of National Drug Control Policy, and the Office of Management and Budget.

Executive Departments Most of the work of the Federal Government is done by the 14 executive departments, each of which is built around some broad field of activity. Each department head serves in the President's Cabinet. The executive departments are the Department of State, the Department of Defense, the Department of Agriculture, the Department of Education, the Department of the Treasury, the Department of Justice, the Department of the Interior, the Department of Commerce, the Department of Labor, the Department of Health and Human Services, the Department of Housing and Urban Development, the Department of Transportation, the Department of Energy, and the Department of Veteran Affairs.

Independent Agencies These agencies are located outside departments and have no Cabinet status. Some examples are the CIA, the Environmental Protection Agency, the U.S. Postal Service, and the Federal Trade Commission.

Key Foreign and Defense Departments and Agencies

Central Intelligence Agency (CIA) A key part of the establishment of foreign policy, the CIA works under the direction of the National Security Council (NSC). The CIA gathers information, analyzes and evaluates data, and briefs the President and NSC about what has been learned.

Defense Department Created to unify the nation's armed forces

Immigration and Naturalization Service (INS) Deals with persons who come to the United States from abroad to live and work and who may become naturalized American citizens

NASA An independent agency created to handle the nation's space programs; NASA's explorations have both military and scientific importance.

Selective Service System Created to institute the draft, or compulsory military service; from 1940 to 1973, a major source of military power

State Department The President's presence in foreign affairs, giving advice on the formulation and conduct of the nation's foreign policy

Presidential Succession

(1) Vice President

(2) Speaker of the House

(3) President *pro tempore* of the Senate

(4) Secretary of State

(5) Secretary of the Treasury

(6) Secretary of Defense

(7) Attorney General

(8) Secretary of the Interior

(9) Secretary of Agriculture

(10) Secretary of Commerce

(11) Secretary of Labor

(12) Secretary of Health and Human Services

(13) Secretary of Housing and Urban Development

(14) Secretary of Transportation

(15) Secretary of Energy

(16) Secretary of Education

(17) Secretary of Veterans Affairs

Taxes

The Constitution underscores the central importance of the power to tax by listing it first among all of the many powers granted to Congress.

Corporate Income Tax	Each corporation is taxed on all its earnings above the cost of doing business.
Custom Duties	A tax is laid on goods brought into the United States from abroad.
Estate and Gift Taxes	The estate tax is imposed on the assets of one who dies, while a gift tax is imposed on the making of a gift by a living person to avoid the estate tax.
Excise Taxes	Excise taxes are laid on the manufacture, sale, or consumption of goods and/or the performance of services—includes taxes on tobacco, liquor, gasoline, firearms, airline tickets, et cetera.
Income Tax	This tax is the largest source of federal revenue today. It is a flexible tax levied on the earnings of both individuals and corporations.
Individual Income Tax	This tax is levied on each person's taxable income—one's total income in the previous year minus certain exemptions and deductions.
Social Insurance Taxes	The Federal Government collects huge sums to finance three social welfare programs: the Old-Age, Survivors, and Disability Insurance (OASDI), Medicare, and the unemployment compensation program.

The Federal Budget

Step 1	Federal agencies send their money requests to the Office of Management and Budget (OMB).
Step 2	The OMB reviews agency requests and melds them into the President's budget. In January or February, the President sends his budget to Congress.
Step 3	Congress reviews budget, enacts several appropriations measures.
Step 4	The President either signs funding measures or vetoes one or more of the funding measures. If the President vetoes one or more of the measures, Congress must get a two-thirds majority to override it. If Congress cannot override the veto, Congress and the President must reach a compromise to resolve the dispute(s).

The United Nations

The General Assembly	Called the "the town meeting of the world." Each member has a seat and a vote. It meets once a year although special sessions may be called.
The Security Council	It bears the responsibility for maintaining international peace. Its measures range from calling on conflicting parties to settle differences peacefully to placing economic and/or military sanctions on offending nations.
The Economic and Social Council (ECOSOC)	It is responsible for carrying out the UN's economic, cultural, educational, health, and related activities. Its specialized agencies are The World Health Organization (WHO), The International Labour Organization (ILO), The International Monetary Fund (IMF), The World Bank Group, The International Fund for Agricultural Development (IFAD), The Food and Agriculture Organization (FAO), The United Nations Industrial Development Organization (UNIDO), The International Civil Aviation Organization (ICAO), The International Maritime Organization (IMO), The International Telecommunications Union (ITU), The Universal Postal Union (UPU), The World Intellectual Property Organization (WIPO), The World Meteorological Organization (WMO), and The United Nations Educational, Scientific, and Cultural Organization (UNESCO)
Trusteeship Council	It promotes the well-being of the peoples of all "non-self-governing territories."
International Court of Justice (ICJ)	This is the UN's judicial arm.
The Secretariat	This is the civil service branch of the UN. It is headed by the secretary-general.

Key Terms

Alien Foreign-born resident; noncitizen

Appellate jurisdiction The authority of a court to review decisions of inferior (lower) courts

Assimilation The process by which people of one culture merge into and become part of another culture

Bail A sum of money that the accused may be required to post (deposit with the court) as a guarantee that he or she will appear in court at the proper time

Bench trial A trial in which the judge alone hears the case

Bill of Attainder A legislative act that inflicts punishment without a court trial

Capital punishment The death penalty

Certificate A method of putting a case before the Supreme Court; used when a lower court is not clear about the procedure or rule of law that should apply in a case and asks the Supreme Court to certify the answer to a specific question

Civil case A case involving a noncriminal matter, such as a contract dispute or a claim of patent infringement

Concurrent jurisdiction Power shared by federal and State courts to hear certain cases

Concurring opinion Written explanation of the views of one or more judges who support a decision reached by a majority of the court but wish to add or emphasize a point that was not made in the majority decision

Content neutral The government can regulate assemblies on the basis of time, place, and manner, but it cannot regulate assemblies on the basis on what might be said

Court-martial A court composed of military personnel for the trial of those accused of violating military law

Criminal case A case in which a defendant is tried for committing a crime as defined by the law

De facto segregation Segregation even if no law requires it

De jure segregation Segregation by law, with legal sanction

Defendant In a civil suit, the person against whom a court action is brought by the plaintiff; in a criminal case, the person charged with the crime

Denaturalization The process through which naturalized citizens may involuntarily lose their citizenship

Deportation A legal process in which aliens are legally required to leave the United States

Dissenting opinion Written explanation of the views of one or more judges who disagree with (dissent from) a decision reached by a majority of the court

Docket A court's list of cases to be heard

Double jeopardy Part of the Fifth Amendment that says that no person can be put in jeopardy of life or limb twice; once a person has been tried for a crime, he or she cannot be tried again for the same crime.

Due Process Clause Part of the Fourteenth Amendment that guarantees that no state can deny basic rights to its people

Establishment Clause Separates church and state

Ex post facto law A law applied to an act committed before the law's passage

Exclusionary rule Evidence gained as the result of an illegal act by police cannot be used against the person from whom it was seized

Exclusive jurisdiction Power of the federal courts alone to hear certain cases

Expatriation The legal process by which a loss of citizenship occurs

Free Exercise Clause The second part of the constitutional guarantee of religious freedom, guaranteeing to each person the right to believe whatever he or she chooses to believe in matters of religion

Grand jury The formal device by which a person can be accused of a serious crime

Heterogeneous Of another or different race, family or kind; composed of a mix of elements

Immigrant Those people legally admitted as permanent residents of a country

Indictment A formal complaint before a grand jury that charges the accused with one or more crimes

Inferior courts The lower federal courts, beneath the Supreme Court

Integration The process of bringing a group into equal membership in society

Involuntary servitude Forced labor

Jim Crow law A law that separates people on the basis of race; aimed primarily at African Americans

Jurisdiction The authority of a court to hear a case

Jus sanguinis The law of blood, which determines citizenship based on one's parents' citizenship

Jus soli The law of soil, which determines citizenship based on where a person is born

Libel False and malicious use of printed words

Majority opinion Officially called the Opinion of the Court; announces the Court's decision in a case and sets out the reasoning upon which it is based

Miranda Rule The constitutional rights that police must read to a suspect before questioning can occur

Original jurisdiction The power of a court to hear a case first, before any other court

Parochial Church-related

Picketing Patrolling of a business site by workers who are on strike

Plaintiff In civil law, the party who brings a suit or some other legal action against another (the defendant) in court

Police power The authority of each State to act to protect and promote the public health, safety, morals, and general welfare of its people

Preventive detention A law that allows federal judges to order that an accused felon be held, without bail, when there is good reason to believe that he or she will commit yet another serious crime before trial

Probable cause Reasonable grounds; a reasonable suspicion of crime

Procedural due process The procedures and the methods of governmental action

Process of incorporation The process of incorporating, or including, most of the guarantees in the Bill of Rights into the Fourteenth Amendment's Due Process Clause

Redress Satisfaction of a claim payment

Refugee One who leaves his or her home to seek protection from war, persecution, or some other danger

Reservation Public land set aside by a government for use by Native American tribes

Reverse discrimination Discrimination against the majority group

Right of association The right to associate with others to promote political, economic, and other social causes

Search warrant A court order authorizing a search

Sedition The crime of attempting to overthrow the government by force or to disrupt its lawful activities by violent acts

Seditious speech The advocating, or urging, of an attempt to overthrow the government by force or to disrupt its lawful activities with violence

Separate-but-equal doctrine A constitutional basis for laws that separate one group from another on the basis of race

Shield law A law that gives reporters some protection against having to disclose their sources or reveal other confidential information in legal proceedings

Slander False and malicious use of spoken words

Substantive due process The substance and the policies of governmental action

Symbolic speech Expression by conduct; communicating ideas through facial expressions, body language, or by carrying a sign or wearing an arm band

Treason Betrayal of one's country; in the Constitution, by levying war against the United States or offering comfort or aid to its enemies

Writ of assistance Blanket search warrant with which British custom officials invaded private homes to search for smuggled goods

Writ of certiorari An order by a higher court directing a lower court to send up the record in a given case for review; from the Latin, meaning "to be more certain"

Writ of habeas corpus A court order that prevents unjust arrests and imprisonment

Structure of the Judiciary Branch

The Constitution created only the Supreme Court, giving Congress the power to create lower, or "inferior," courts as needed. Other than the Supreme Court, there are two separate court systems in the United States. The national judiciary spans the country with its more than 100 courts, and each of the 50 states has its own system of courts.

- **Supreme Court** Highest court in the land, created by the Constitution
- **Constitutional Courts** Created by Congress to exercise "the judicial Power of the United States"; they include the courts of appeals, the district courts, and the U.S. Court of International Trade.
  - **U.S. courts of appeals** Established to relieve the Supreme Court of much of the burden of hearing appeals from the district courts
  - **U.S. courts of appeals for the Federal circuit** The federal appeals courts
  - **District courts** The federal trial courts
  - **U.S. Court of International Trade** Hears civil cases arising out of tariff and other trade-related laws

- **Special Courts** The special courts do not exercise the broad "judicial Power of the United States." Rather, they have been created by Congress to hear specific kinds of cases.
  - **U.S. Court of Appeals for the Armed Forces** A civilian tribunal that is entirely separate from the military establishment
  - **U.S. Court of Appeals for Veterans Claims** Hears cases in which individuals claim that the VA has denied or otherwise mishandled valid claims for veterans' benefits
  - **U.S. Court of Federal Claims** Set up to hear claims against the United States government
  - **U.S. Courts District of Columbia** Provide a judicial system for the nation's capital
  - **Territorial Courts** Courts created for the nation's territories
  - **U.S. Tax Court** Hears civil but not criminal cases involving disputes over the application of the tax laws

UNIT 5 — THE JUDICIAL BRANCH *(continued)*

Civil Liberties

Civil liberties are the guarantees of the safety of persons, opinions, and property from the arbitrary acts of government; include freedom of speech and freedom of religion.

- **Due Process of Law** The Federal Government cannot deprive any person of "life, liberty, or property, without due process of law." The Fourteenth Amendment places that same restriction on State and local governments as well. The government must act fairly and in accord with established rules in whatever it does.

- **Freedom and Security of the Person** Several of the Constitution's guarantees are intended to protect the right of every American to live in freedom, to be free of physical restraints, to be secure in his or her person, and to be secure in his or her home.

- **Freedom of Assembly and Petition** The Constitution protects the right of the people to assemble to express their views on public matters. It also protects the people's right to bring their views to the attention of public officials by such varied means as written petitions, letters, or advertisements; lobbying; or parades, marches, or other demonstrations.

- **Freedom of Religion** The Bill of Rights provides first for the protection of religious liberty. The First and Fourteenth Amendments provide "a wall of separation between church and state" and prohibit any arbitrary interference by government in "the free exercise" of religion.

- **Freedom of Speech and the Press** The guarantees of free speech and press in the First and Fourteenth Amendments serve two fundamentally important purposes: 1) to guarantee each person a right of free expression and 2) to guarantee to all persons a full, wide-ranging discussion of public affairs.

- **Rights of the Accused** The law intends that any person who is suspected or accused of a crime must be presumed innocent until proven guilty by fair and lawful means. Laws prohibit unjust arrests and imprisonment, punishment without a court trial, and being tried twice for the same crime and provide the right to a speedy and public trial, and a trial by jury if accused of a federal crime, and the right to an adequate defense. Suspects must be informed of their rights before questioning.

Civil Rights Laws and Policies

Civil rights are those positive acts of government that seek to make constitutional guarantees a reality for all people.

- **Affirmative Action** A federal policy that requires employers to remedy the effects of past discriminations by filling certain numbers of jobs with people of minority backgrounds or females to meet a quota

- **Civil Rights Act of 1964** Safeguarded the right to vote and outlawed discrimination in the areas of public accommodation, programs that receive federal funding, and employment

- **Civil Rights Act of 1968** With minor exceptions, forbids anyone to refuse to sell or rent a dwelling to any person on grounds of race, color, religion, national origin, gender, or disability

Requirements for Citizenship

A citizen is a member of a state or nation who owes allegiance to it by birth or naturalization and is entitled to full civil rights.

The requirements for acquiring citizenship through naturalization are:

1. Be at least 18 years old
2. Have entered the country legally, lived in the United States for at least five years, and been a resident in certain States for at least three months
3. File a petition for naturalization with the clerk of a Federal district court or a State court of record
4. Be literate in the English language
5. Be "of good moral character," "attached to the principles of the Constitution," and "well disposed to the good order and happiness of the United States"
6. Have "a knowledge and understanding of the fundamentals of the history, and the principles and form of government, of the United States"
7. Take an oath or affirmation in which the applicant absolutely renounces any allegiance to any foreign power and promises to "support and defend the Constitution and laws of the United States against all enemies, foreign and domestic"

Key Terms

Autonomous Independent

Bourgeoisie The social class between the aristocracy and the proletariat class; the middle class

By-election A special election held to choose a replacement for a member of parliament in the event of a death

Capital All the human-made resources that are used to produce goods and services

Capitalist Someone who owns capital and puts it to productive use; often applied to people who own large businesses

Centrally planned economy A system in which government bureaucrats plan how an economy will develop over a period of years

Coalition A temporary alliance of several groups who come together to form a working majority and so to control a government

Collectivization Collective or state ownership of the means of production

Common law An unwritten law that is made by a judge and that has developed over centuries from those generally accepted ideas of right and wrong that have gained judicial recognition

Commune A large grouping of several collective farms

Consensus General agreement among various groups on fundamental matters; broad agreement on public questions

Cultural Revolution Begun in 1966, Mao Zedong's Red Guards attacked, bullied, and "reeducated" teachers, intellectuals, and anyone else who seemed to lack revolutionary fervor

Devolution The delegation of authority from the central government to regional governments

Dissolution The power of the Prime Minister to dissolve the House of Representatives

Entrepreneur An individual with the drive and ambition to combine land, labor, and capital resources to produce goods or offer services

Factors of production Basic resources which are used to make all goods and services

Five-year plan A plan that projects economic development over the next five years

Free enterprise system Investments that are determined by private decision rather than by state control, and determined in a free market

Glasnost The Soviet policy of openness under which tolerance of dissent and freedom of expression increased

Gosplan A large agency in the Soviet Union, introduced by Stalin, to run centralized planning

Great Leap Forward The five-year plan for 1958 which was an attempt to quickly modernize China

Laissez-faire theory A theory that suggests that government should play a very limited role in society

Law of supply and demand A law which states that when supplies of goods and services become plentiful, prices tend to drop

Market economy Economic system in which decisions on production and consumption of goods and services are based on voluntary exchange of markets

Mestizo A person with both Spanish or Portuguese and Native American ancestry

Minister Cabinet member, most commonly of the House of Commons

Monarchy A government head by a hereditary ruler

Monopoly A firm that is the only source of a product or service

Nationalization The governmental acquisition of private industry for public use

North American Free Trade Agreement (NAFTA) An agreement that removed trade restrictions among the United States, Canada, and Mexico, thus increasing cross-border trade

Perestroika The restructuring of political and economic life under the rule of Mikhail Gorbachev

Prefecture The 47 political subdivisions into which Japan is divided

Privatization The process of returning national enterprises to private ownership

Proletariat The working class

Purge A purification

Shadow cabinet Members of opposition parties who watch, or shadow, particular Cabinet members and would be ready to run the government

Soviets A government council, elected by and representing the people

Trust A device by which several corporations in the same line of business combine to eliminate competition and regulate prices

Welfare state Countries that provide extensive social services at little or no cost to the users

U N I T 6 — COMPARATIVE POLITICAL AND ECONOMIC SYSTEMS *(continued)*

Types of Economic Systems

Capitalism (market economy)	An economic system based on the idea of free enterprise, characterized by private or corporate ownership of capital goods (physical capital) and investments that are determined by private decision rather than by state control.
Communism	An ideology that calls for the collective, or state, ownership of land and other productive property. Communist systems depend on a strong central government that owns all industry and farmland and plans all parts of the national economy.
Socialism (centrally planned economy)	A philosophy based on the idea that the benefits of economic activity should be fairly distributed. Socialist governments strive for social and economic equality for all members of society.

Types of Political Systems

Political System	Country	Characteristics
Communist	China	Government dominated by the Communist Party, which exerts direct control over local political subdivisions; National People's Congress and the State Council form the national government; nationwide system of "people's courts" deal with both criminal and civil cases
Parliamentary Democracy	Great Britain	Unitary government based on an unwritten constitution; hereditary monarch reigns but does not rule; bicameral Parliament holds judicial and executive power; recently began a process of devolution, or the delegation of authority to regional governments
Parliamentary Democracy	Japan	Constitution written with American guidance after World War II; legislature, the National Diet, consists of the House of Councillors and the House of Representatives; prime minister and cabinet are chosen by and responsible to the House of Representatives; independent judicial system
Constitutional Representative	Mexico	Government includes an executive branch headed by the president, a bicameral legislature, and a national judiciary
Post-Communist Democracy	Russia	1993 constitution set out plan for government and guarantees individual rights; one-party system of Soviet era replaced by a multiparty system; powers separated between executive branch (president) and legislative branch (the bicameral Federal Assembly)

Comparison of Governments

	Great Britain	Japan	Mexico	Russia	China
Type	constitutional monarchy	constitutional monarchy	federal republic	federation	communist state
Chief of State	monarch	emperor	president	president	president
Head of Government	prime minister	prime minister	president	premier	premier
Executive Branch	prime minister is head of majority party in the House of Commons	prime minister designated by the National Diet	president elected by popular vote for a six-year term	president elected for four-year term; premier appointed by president	president elected by National People's Congress for a five-year term; premier nominated by president, confirmed by National People's Congress
Legislative Branch	bicameral Parliament	bicameral National Diet	bicameral National Congress	bicameral Federal Assembly	unicameral National People's Congress
Judicial Branch	Crown Court	Supreme Court	Supreme Court of Justices	Constitutional Court, Supreme Court, Superior Court of Arbitration	Supreme People's Court

© Pearson Education, Inc.

Factors of Production

Land	Includes all natural resources. It has a variety of economic uses—agriculture, mining, forestry. Along with farms and property, economists include water in rivers and lakes and the coal, iron, and petroleum.
Labor	The men and women who work in mines, factories, offices, hospitals, et cetera.
Capital	All the human-made resources used to produce goods and services. Physical capital includes money, buildings, machines, computers. Human capital includes knowledge and skills that workers gain from the work experience.

Factors of Free Enterprise System

Private ownership	Private individuals and companies own most of the means of production—the resources used to produce goods and services. Individuals also own the right to their labor.
Individual initiative	All individuals are free to start, run, and dissolve their own businesses.
Profit	Individuals are entitled to benefit from whatever their investment or enterprise earns or gains in value.
Competition	A situation in which a number of companies offer the same product or service. Competition often helps to hold down prices and keep quality high. It promotes efficiency. The laws of supply and demand determines prices.

Types of Business Organizations under Capitalism

Sole proprietorship	A business owned by a single individual. It is the most flexible form of business organization. It is only limited by the owner's ability to contribute and manage the business.
Partnership	A partnership is a business owned by two or more individuals.
Corporation	A corporation includes both small companies and large national firms. It has many owners called shareholders and exists as its own legal entity—a corporation enjoys the same legal status as a person.

Characteristics of Social Economies

Nationalization	Places enterprises under governmental control. Its goal is to give each worker a say in deciding how companies are run.
Public welfare	Aims to provide for the equal distribution of necessities and services.
Taxation	Tends to place most of the burden on the upper and middle classes.
Centrally planned economy	Government bureaucrats plan how an economy will develop over a period of years.

Characteristics of Communist Economies

Role of Communist Party	Holds the decision-making power in both the government and the economy. Its party leaders hold top government positions.
Central planning	Bureaucrats plan and supervise production in factories, farms, and stores. A five-year plan sets economic goals that dictate growth in industry and agriculture.
Collectivization	Merges small private farms into large government-owned agriculture enterprises.
State ownership	The state owns industrial enterprises, transportation, and other parts of the economy.

Key Terms

Budget A financial plan for the use of money, personnel, and property

Civil law The portion of the law relating to human conduct, to disputes between private parties, and to disputes between private parties and government not covered by criminal law

Clemency Mercy or leniency granted to an offender by a chief executive

Constituent power The nonlegislative power of Constitution-making and the constitutional amendment process

Factors of production Basic resources that are used to make all goods and services

Felony A serious crime that may be punished by a heavy fine and/or imprisonment or even death

Fundamental law Laws of basic and lasting importance that may not easily be changed

Incorporation The process by which a State establishes a city as a legal body

Information A formal charge filed by a prosecutor without the action of a grand jury

Initiative A process in which a certain number of qualified voters sign petitions in favor of a proposal, which then goes directly to the ballot

Item veto A governor may veto one or more items in a bill without rejecting the entire measure

Jury A body of persons selected according to law who hear evidence and decide questions of fact in a court case

Justice of the Peace A judge who stands on the lowest level of the State judicial system and presides over justice courts

Limited government Basic principle of American government that states that government is restricted in what it may do and that each individual has rights that government cannot take away

Magistrate A justice who handles minor civil complaints and misdemeanor cases that arise in an urban setting

Metropolitan area A city and the area around it

Misdemeanor A lesser offense, punishable by a small fine and/or a short jail term

Pardon Release from the punishment or legal consequences of a crime by the President (in a federal case) or a governor (in a State case)

Parole The release of a prisoner short of the complete term of the original sentence

Police power The authority of each State to act to protect and promote the public health, safety, morals, and general welfare of its people

Popular sovereignty Basic principle of the American system of government that asserts that the people are the source of any and all governmental power and that government can exist only with the consent of the governed

Preliminary hearing The first step in a major criminal prosecution during which the judge decides if the evidence is enough to hold the person for action by the grand jury or the prosecutor

Recall A petition procedure by which voters may remove an elected official from office before the completion of his or her regular term

Referendum A process by which a legislative measure is referred to the State's voters for final approval or rejection

Reprieve An official postponement of the execution of a sentence

Statutory law A law passed by the legislature

Strong-mayor government A type of government in which the mayor heads the city's administration

Urbanization The percentage of the population of a State living in cities of more than 250,000 people or in suburbs with more than 50,000 people

Warrant A court order authorizing, or making legal, some official action, such as a search warrant or an arrest warrant

Weak-mayor government A type of government in which the mayor shares his or her executive duties with other elected officials

Zoning The practice of dividing a city into a number of districts and regulating the uses to which property in each of them may be put

Direct Legislative Process

Initiative	Voters in 17 States can propose constitutional amendments. In 27 States, voters can propose ordinary statutes. A certain number of qualified voters must sign initiative petitions to propose a law. In a direct initiative, the measure goes directly to the ballot. This is the most common initiative. In an indirect initiative, the proposal goes to the legislature where it approves or disapproves of it.
Referendum	A mandatory referendum requires that the legislature refers a measure to the voters. An optional referendum measure is one that the legislature refers to the voters voluntarily. Under the popular referendum, the people may demand via a petition that a measure passed by the legislature be referred to them for final action.

Levels of Local Government

City Incorporated body that provides public services as described in a charter; may have one of three basic forms of government: a mayor-council, a commission, or a council-manager form of government.

- **Mayor-council government** The oldest and most widely used type of city government—an elected mayor as the chief executive and an elected council as its legislative body
- **Commission government** A government formed by commissioners, heads of different departments of city government, who are popularly elected to form the city council and thus center both legislative and executive powers in one body
- **Council-manager government** A modification of the mayor-council government, it consists of a strong council of members elected on a non-partisan ballot, a weak mayor, elected by the people, and a manager, named by the council

County Major unit of local government in most States; created by the State

Municipality Urban political unit within a township that exists as a separate governmental entity

Special District An independent unit created to perform one or more related governmental functions at the local level

Town In New England, the major unit of local government; includes all of the rural and the urban areas within its boundaries; delivers most of the services that are the responsibility of cities and counties elsewhere in the country

Township Subdivision of a county; functions tend to be rural

Organization of State Government

A state's constitution is the supreme law of the state and sets out the ways in which the government of the State is organized. State constitutions distribute power among the various branches of the State government, authorizing and placing limits on the exercise of power. A state's constitution is subordinate to the Constitution of the United States.

- **Judicial** Courts decide disputes between private persons and between private persons and the government and exercise power of judicial review and check the conduct of all the other agencies of both State and local government.
- **Governor** Principal executive officer of each State as well as legislator, party leader, opinion leader, and ceremonial figure
- **State Administration** Other elected officials and officers who share the control of the governor's administration; includes lieutenant governor, attorney general, secretary of state, and treasurer
- **State Legislature** Lawmaking body of the State government, responsible for translating the public will into the State's public policy; members elected from districts within the State

Key Principles of State Constitutions

Basic principles	Built on principles of popular sovereignty and limited government. Pledges the preservation of a republican form of government.
Protections of civil rights	Includes a bill of rights that lists the rights that individuals hold against the State and its officers and agencies.
Governmental structure	Every State constitution deals with the structure of government at both the State and local levels.
Governmental powers and processes	Lists the powers vested in the three branches of government.
Constitutional change	Can be altered through a revision or an amendment process.
Miscellaneous provisions	Additional information including the preamble and "dead letter" provisions

Methods Used to Change a State Constitution

Convention	• Constitutional conventions are used most often to revise existing constitutions and to write new ones. • Every State legislature can call a constitutional convention, subject to voter approval.
Legislature	• Most constitutional amendments are proposed by the legislature. • The process varies among the States; the simpler the process, the more amendments are proposed and adopted.
Initiative	In some States, voters can propose amendments: • A specified number of voters must sign a petition. • The proposal goes to the ballot. • The people approve or reject the amendment.

Kinds of Law Applied in State Courts

Constitutional law	The highest form of law in this country is based on the provisions of the United States Constitution and the State constitutions and on judicial interpretation of these documents.
Statutory law	Consists of statutes enacted by legislative bodies.
Administrative law	Composed of the rules, orders, and regulations that are issued by federal, State, or local executive officers.
Common law	Covers nearly all aspects of human conduct.
Equity	Supplements common law. Developed when remedies under common law did not provide fairness, justice, and right.

The Jury System

Jury	A body of persons selected according to law who hear evidence and decide questions of fact in a court case.
Grand jury	Determines whether the evidence against a person charged with a crime is sufficient to justify a trial. It is used almost exclusively in criminal proceedings.
Information	A formal charge filed by the prosecutor without the action of a grand jury.
Petit jury	In either criminal or civil cases, reviews the evidence and decides the disputed facts.
Selection of jury	Depending upon the State, the lists are drawn from poll books, county tax rolls, motor vehicle and drivers license lists, and/or public utility and telephone company billings.

Types of Taxes

Business taxes	These include severance taxes—levies on the removal of natural resources—license taxes, documentary and stock transfer taxes, and capital stock taxes.
Estate tax	This is a tax levied directly on the full estate of one who dies.
Income tax	This is a tax levied on the income of individuals and/or corporations.
Inheritance tax	This is a tax levied on the beneficiary's share of an estate.
Other taxes	These include payroll taxes, amusement taxes, and license taxes for nonbusiness purposes such as hunting, fishing, and marriage.
Progressive tax	This is a type of tax proportionate to income.
Property tax	This is a tax levied on real and personal property.
Regressive tax	This is a tax levied at a flat rate, without regard to the level of a taxpayer's income or ability to pay.
Sales tax	This is a tax placed on the sale of various commodities, paid by the purchaser.